M000222605

"*Unteachable Lessons* le ... journeys into grief, into silence, into trust, ... ... of all, the journey into God. No one can take these adventures for us—but Carl McColman is a wise and caring companion on the path. Highly recommended."

— Richard Rohr, OFM, author of *The Universal Christ*

"Riveting, inspiring and beautifully written, a moving account of finding God amidst both the laughter and tears in life."

— James Martin, SJ, author of *Jesus: A Pilgrimage*

"Carl McColman's first gift is his commitment to write about things that matter. His second gift is his ability to write about them with clarity and warmth, enticing his readers to go places with him that we might otherwise not have gone. In this book he leads us to the brink of lessons no book can teach, then frees us to go forward to learn them, trusting the God who meets us at every step on the unknown way."

— Barbara Brown Taylor, author of *Holy Envy: Finding God in the Faith of Others*

"These lively stories of loss, awakening, and moments of divine encounter and surprise offer invitations at every turn to recognize how the Spirit lives and moves in our own lives as well as in the author's. Deft and funny, rich with spiritual insight and unpretentiously articulate, this book is one to be enjoyed, dog-eared, carried to retreats, and shared."

— Marilyn McEntyre, author of *When Poets Pray*

"We have come to expect inspiring and sure-footed guidance from the pen of Carl McColman. In this beautifully written memoir, McColman continues his sound guidance through wide learning, deep experience, and the humor of the truly wise."

— Martin Laird, OSA, author of *An Ocean of Light*

"This powerful little book inspires and instructs masterfully. A must-read for those interested in truths beneath the words."

— Margaret Benefiel, author of *Soul at Work*
and *The Soul of a Leader*

"*Unteachable Lessons* is an invitation to dance—with life, with the Holy Spirit, with the mystery of unknowing. It is a treasure that will require you to join the dance, not just read the words."

— Therese Taylor-Stinson, founder
of the Spiritual Directors of Color Network and
editor of *Ain't Gonna Let Nobody Turn Me Around:*
*Stories of Contemplation and Justice*

8/21

# UNTEACHABLE
# LESSONS

Why Wisdom Can't Be Taught
(and Why That's Okay)

Carl McColman

WILLIAM B. EERDMANS PUBLISHING COMPANY
GRAND RAPIDS, MICHIGAN

Wm. B. Eerdmans Publishing Co.
4035 Park East Court SE, Grand Rapids, Michigan 49546
www.eerdmans.com

Published 2019
Printed in the United States of America

25  24  23  22  21  20  19      1  2  3  4  5  6  7

ISBN 978-0-8028-7575-4

**Library of Congress Cataloging-in-Publication Data**

Names: McColman, Carl, author.
Title: Unteachable lessons : why wisdom can't be taught (and why
    that's okay) / Carl McColman.
Description: Grand Rapids : Eerdmans Publishing Co., 2019. |
    Includes bibliographical references.
Identifiers: LCCN 2019017684 | ISBN 9780802875754 (pbk. : alk.
    paper)
Subjects: LCSH: Spirituality—Christianity—Study and teaching.
Classification: LCC BV4511 .M43 2019 | DDC 248.2—dc23
LC record available at https://lccn.loc.gov/2019017684

*For Cassidy and Kevin*

No thought, no mental effort will teach us anything about pure love. We can learn of it only through the activity of God, and God teaches us, both through our reason and through difficulties and setbacks.

Jean-Pierre de Caussade,
*Abandonment to Divine Providence*

It is not enough to have bookish knowledge about spiritual things.

John Wright,
quoted in *The Friend of the Bridegroom*

# CONTENTS

# FOREWORD

In Chapter 1 of *Unteachable Lessons*, you'll meet its author, Carl, and you'll meet Fran, his wife. You'll also meet Rhiannon, their daughter, and Rhiannon will steal the show. You won't forget her, I promise.

As you read words about Rhiannon, Fran, and Carl, you'll feel something, see something, know something that can't be put into words. In that way, you'll not only understand how some lessons are unteachable, you'll also experience it. And that's only in the first chapter.

In Chapter 2, you'll read one of the best descriptions of a spiritual experience I've come across, one that tries to capture in words something that, obviously, can't be. And whether you have had or ever will have a similar experience, you'll be enriched by Carl's telling of it. You may, to some degree, catch something beyond words through his words.

In Chapter 3, Carl will become something of a matchmaker, introducing you to his coy friend Communal Silence to see if the two of you might fall in love. Be careful—you may.

And the following chapters will similarly introduce you to things you already know, but then again, don't. Your body. The relationship between prayer and kissing. The relationship between fear and trust.

Don't tell anyone this (including yourself), because it might scare them (and you) away: all of these lessons are lessons in spirituality, or the contemplative life, or (I hesitate to say the word) *mysticism*. You wouldn't necessarily know this if I hadn't told you, because Carl's style of writing is so down-to-earth, so honest, human, and normal, that it won't feel like anything ghost-y or Spirit-y at all.

And that's exactly as it should be.

All this will make perfect sense when Carl ends this book, not with a deep meditation on some profound tome by Thomas Merton or Julian of Norwich or Augustine, but on his favorite Dr. Seuss book.

One last thing. As a writer myself, I know the temptation of going on and on. A lot of us writers love writing more than our readers love reading. But this is a short book, short and delicious. And nutritious. And so it won't satiate your appetite for words. In fact, it will do the opposite.

BRIAN D. MCLAREN

# Prologue: A Cat by the Tail

I'd like to share with you a story that shows up from time to time in my email inbox or my social media feed. I don't know if this actually happened or if it is a myth. If it really happened, I couldn't tell you where or when. But if it is a myth, that's okay, for like all great myths it is still a true story, in the deepest (if not literal) sense of the word.

The story goes that a gathering of Buddhist and Christian authors and monastics took place. The authors—an assortment of theologians and dharma teachers representing a variety of lineages and traditions—held a conference where they delivered papers and engaged in various conversations concerning interreligious dialogue. In a separate but nearby building, the monks and nuns also came together, where they devoted most of their time to meditation and contemplation.

By the end of the week, both groups gathered for a closing interfaith ceremony. It became obvious to all who were present that the various authors, while polite and civil toward each other, had not really formed any kind of relationships, at least beyond their professional collegiality. On the other hand, the various monastics were all hugging one another, filled with warmth, smiles, and a clear sense of bonded charity—as if they had been friends for ages.

When I lived in Washington, DC, I took several classes on Christian meditation—what others might call contemplation or silent prayer—at the Shalem Institute for Spiritual Formation. In Shalem's library hung an old framed print featuring a Quaker proverb: "Speak only when your words are an improvement upon silence."

Some fifteen hundred years ago, Saint Benedict said something similar in his *Holy Rule*: "There are times when good words are to be left unsaid, out of esteem for silence."[1]

What Benedict and the Quakers—let alone the monks and nuns from our little interfaith story—are trying to say is simply this: sometimes words get in the way.

This is a very alarming thought for people who make their living, like I do, from writing and speaking.

In the Christian faith, language, which is to say words—or at least *the* Word—occupies a place of almost singular honor. We do more than merely believe in God—we believe in a God who speaks. *He Is There and He Is Not Silent*, proclaimed the title of a book by a famous twentieth-century evangelical, Francis Schaeffer.[2]

The Christian God is a God who talks. And this God-talk reaches its zenith with the incarnation of Jesus Christ, the second person of the Holy Trinity, the Son of God, who is indeed one with God, the *Logos*, the Word of God.

Spirituality invites us to imitate God, and it's obvious Christians worship a God who talks, for we are likewise a very chatty bunch. Even when God is not talking to us, we're busy doing plenty of our own talking. We talk *to* God (prayer), and we talk *about* God (theology). Literally hundreds of thousands of books on theology have been written over the ages. Not only do we mortals love a talking God, but we sure love having God to talk about, too.

If language is good enough for God, why should monks and nuns and Quakers run around telling us to be silent?

I'm not sure I can answer that question *because the answer can't be put into words.*

Every time I sit down to write about silence, I just get amused by the sheer irony of it all. But over the years, in between writing books and a blog and various opportunities to speak and teach and lead retreats, I've come to recognize something that is very humbling: at its heart, Christian spirituality and faith simply cannot be taught. The lessons of spirituality are unteachable lessons.

Now, I don't want to suggest that God has made a mistake by giving us Jesus the Word or that the Bible is somehow deficient because it is filled with all sorts of words. (Here's a fun bit of trivia: the Old and the New Testaments contain a combined total of well over ten thousand unique words.)

3

I don't mean to imply that verbal communication is somehow bad or even deficient. But some things simply cannot be communicated by words or at least cannot be communicated as well by words. Words are the map, not the territory; they are the finger pointing to the moon, not the moon itself.

You could even say this about Jesus: as the Word of God, Jesus shares with us not only himself but also the One who sent him: One whom even the Word of God ultimately cannot put into words.

Mark Twain is supposed to have said that a person who carries a cat by the tail learns something that cannot be learned any other way.[3] That pretty much sums up what I'm trying to say here.

Fortunately, not all unteachable lessons are of a cat-by-the-tail variety. Some unteachable lessons involve wonder or rapture or joy. They involve moments of time (or of eternity) that cannot be put into words, indeed, cannot even be put into thought. But stumble across one of those moments and you'll never be the same. When you learn a lesson that can never be taught, don't try to teach anyone else, either. Maybe the best you can do is tell your story or point somebody in a direction and say, "this way."

N. T. Wright, in one of his books, recounts the story of a renowned ballerina. "After one of her great performances somebody had the temerity to ask her what her dances *meant*. Her reply was simple and speaks volumes to us: "If I could have said it," she said, "I wouldn't have needed to dance it."[4]

In the pages to come I'm going to tell a few stories, reflect on a few ideas, and share some Scripture with you. Why? Because I hope it will inspire you to dance.

# The Unteachable Lessons

In the movie *Rain Man*, Tom Cruise portrays a self-involved young man named Charlie Babbitt.

When I saw that movie, I realized, to my chagrin, that I'm a lot like Charlie.

Okay, so I don't look nearly as good as Tom Cruise, and my road-worn Subaru seems pretty frumpy compared to the Lamborghinis that Charlie Babbitt sells. But let me explain how I could see myself reflected in his eyes.

Charlie Babbitt's life pretty much revolves around himself, and he likes it that way. Then, one day, he learns that his wealthy (and estranged) father has died, having left the bulk of his multimillion dollar estate to Charlie's institutionalized, autistic savant brother, Raymond (played by Dustin Hoffmann). This is the setup for a picaresque, cross-country adventure, motivated by Charlie's greed; he sets out to use his brother as a pawn to try to gain control of the estate. Charlie clearly sees Raymond as just one big problem and treats him accordingly.

But—spoiler alert—Raymond's vulnerability slowly wins over Charlie's heart.

When I say I'm a lot like Charlie Babbitt, I'm not talking about money or glamour, but rather I'm someone who is rather slow when it comes to learning how to love. Like Charlie, I sailed through my youth pretty much focused only on myself, until a family member forced me to look in the mirror. My saving angel wasn't an autistic brother but a chronically ill little girl.

### "So Happy to Meet You!"

I met Rhiannon on a Monday evening after a weekend camping trip where I had met her mother. By that point Fran had been a single mom for about five years and was tired of men who, as she put it, "just wanted to play." But when we met, the spark was too big to miss, and so when I insisted that I wanted to see her again, she invited me over for dinner—which, I soon realized, was an audition. She greeted me at the door to her kitchen, and when I offered to help, she directed me instead into the living room. "Read Rhiannon a story," she said; it was not a request so much as a command.

On the couch sat a small girl, far too little for her almost seven years. Stunted by polycystic kidney disease, her body and her mind both compromised by a stroke she suffered when only three years old. Now paralyzed on her right side and with only limited motor skills on her left, she was propped in the corner of the sofa, surrounded by pillows to keep from toppling over. She had an angelic face and a big smile, her features clearly asymmetrical thanks to the damage of her brain injury. Still, plenty of light shone in her eyes, and when her mom introduced us, Rhiannon seemed to decide immediately that we were friends.

I, on the other hand, was scared to death.

I barely knew how to comport myself with perfectly healthy children. But someone with the challenges of this tyke? I was in way over my head. Several Dr. Seuss books were strewn on the coffee table and I picked one up—I don't recall which one—and started to read. It soon became obvious that Rhiannon was barely, if at all, interested in the story. However, she was beyond fascinated with *me*.

"I'm so happy to meet you," she said, and oblivious to any kind of personal-space boundaries, she reached over to me as soon as I sat next to her and started to tug, then caress, then tug again, on my beard.

Thus began the most surreal of interactions. I would read the book, and whenever I paused or turned a page, she would tug again at my beard and announce once more, "I'm so happy to meet you." I couldn't decide whether this was annoying or endearing, and in truth it was a little of each. Later, Fran would explain to me that parroting and repetition were typical markers of someone with Rhiannon's brain injury, which among other consequences limited her facility with language. At the moment, unsure how to react, I just kept smiling every time she announced, with eyes glowing, "I'm so happy to meet you."

I must have passed the audition, for Fran kissed me goodbye that night after putting Rhiannon to bed, and made plans to see me the following weekend. I lived 150 miles away, so we began an interstate romance, paying exorbitant phone bills (this was the early nineties when the phone companies still charged for long distance calls by the minute) and seeing each other most weekends. Often Rhiannon would stay with her grandmother on the weekends, allowing us lovebirds a private courtship. So I really didn't fully understand, or face, the unending unendingness of long-term caregiving until, fourteen months after we met, Fran and I got married, and the three of us set out to form a family.

The good news was that by then Rhiannon and I really *were* friends, and while I hadn't quite figured out the stepdad thing, we discovered that we both had basically playful personalities and could make a sport out of egging each other on, whether *on* meant singing silly songs, making funny faces or noises, or playacting our favorite Disney characters. We soon decided that our family was a real-life reenactment of *The Jungle Book*: Rhiannon, naturally, was Mowgli in female form, while her mother was the caring if slightly overresponsible Bagheera. Me? I was Baloo, of course; the great big hippie bear (although sometimes we'd mix it up and I'd get to be King Louie).[1]

After the honeymoon ended and with the flurry of activity as we set up house and I settled into my new job, the weeks started to roll on by—then barely three months after Fran and I were married, her mother got sick. Some unexplained bleeding led to a cancer diagnosis—and an emergency hysterectomy. Fran naturally was distraught and began making plans to drive the seventy-five miles to her mom's hometown to be by her side during surgery.

Clueless, I remained oblivious to what was really going down. My grandparents all died either before I was born or when I was a small child, and my parents were still healthy when Fran and I married. I had no experience dealing with family members facing serious illness and had never read the memo about what it means to be caring and compassionate in those circumstances.

Charlie Babbitt, remember?

When it dawned on Fran that I wasn't particularly motivated to drive with her to the hospital, she said, "Fine, you can stay here and take care of Rhiannon. I should be back in a couple of days."

Gee, I didn't recall *that* being part of the wedding vows. And when I said something to that effect, matters quickly escalated until I was screaming at her—and she was sobbing in the bathroom.

Thankfully, we were attending the Episcopal church where we got married, and one of us managed to pull ourselves together to call a priest, who talked some sense into me—to get me to understand that any decent husband would be doing far more than the little that Fran was asking of me. Furthermore, the priest invited (or perhaps instructed) us to come to see her at the office as soon as possible after Fran got back into town. We did, and walked out of there with a referral to a family therapist.

### "You Have a Choice"

I wish I could say that after that initial fight, and more than a few helpful therapy sessions, I promptly managed to grow up enough to be the kind of husband and step-father that Fran and Rhiannon deserved. And maybe to some extent I did. But the Charlie Babbitt in me died hard. Over the next twenty years, I spent far too much time feeling resentment toward Rhiannon for being sick and needing so much care, and toward Fran for quite sensibly organizing her life around taking care of Rhiannon's complex needs.

I did manage to take some baby steps along the way. Thankfully, my mother-in-law's emergency surgery proved successful and cancer never revisited her. About a year later, when Fran decided to take a series of classes—first to get her teaching certificate and later to burnish her skills as an artist—Rhiannon and I turned our mom-less evenings into adventures. Therapy helped me and Fran to learn how to communicate our needs and requests to one another without triggering either her fear of abandonment or my fear of engulfment. I completed a crash course in every aspect of special-needs daddyhood, from the mundane (transferring Rhiannon from her bed to her wheelchair) to the critical (preparing her array of nightly medicines) to the joyful (taking her Christmas shopping or escorting her to her middle school homecoming).

But the long shadow of my Babbitt-like selfishness was never far away, and for years I nursed a sense of being constrained or finding Rhiannon's never-ending needs for basic care or repeated hospital visits to be, well, just a big fat inconvenience to me.

It's embarrassing as hell to write this, but it's the truth.

After she graduated from high school, I campaigned for Rhiannon to be placed in a group home; I was out-voted 2-1. I honestly thought Rhiannon would benefit from the independence (but the Charlie Babbitt in me just wanted to have an empty nest, for heaven's sake). Fran intuitively recognized that Rhiannon's medical issues were so complex—and her emotional needs likewise complicated, thanks to the stroke—that in all likelihood Rhiannon living anywhere other than home would mean, simply, a significant reduction in the quality of her care.

Honest enough to recognize that this was probably true, I gritted my teeth and accepted that we were in it for the long haul.

Rhiannon and I always remained friends, but as she entered her teen years the turmoil of adolescence came roaring into our lives, gloriously unfiltered thanks to her stroke-injured brain and my persistent self-centeredness. Even a minor conflict could quickly escalate to her screaming "I *hate* you; I wish you weren't my dad!" and me snarling back, "That could be arranged!"

Fran learned a new role: peacemaker, sometimes having to send each of us to opposite ends of the house in the hopes that sooner or later we would both calm down enough to manage our conflict with some small measure of grace. Rhiannon figured out that when she got mad enough, she could yell "All you care about is your writing!" and it would be a direct hit. I know that shouting matches are the common coin of families with teenagers—except that in our case, usually an hour after being told we were hated (yes, sometimes Fran got it too), we would be helping her transfer on and off the toilet. It was amazing training in learning to be fully grounded in the present moment. No grudges, no time for resentment.

Along with the joys and challenges of our shared family life, Rhiannon's complex medical issues never went away. One terrifying summer she developed varices in her esophagus, leading to frightening episodes where she vomited blood. Two weeks in the hospital and then a series of endoscopies ensued, as the doctor literally patched up her wounded esophagus using ligatures. Migraine headaches (an unhappy inheritance from her mother) and dramatic mood swings caused Rhiannon much distress. Eventually it became obvious that she had profound systemic problems related to her kidney disease and resultant problems with her liver and spleen. When a doctor told Fran that Rhiannon would not likely live past the age of thirty, Fran came home and sobbed on my shoulder.

We had Rhiannon evaluated for a transplant, but her problems were too complex. In the brutally candid words of the evaluating surgeon, "A transplant would likely increase, rather than decrease, the risk of mortality within a year." Her kidney specialist, one of the world's premier authorities on polycystic kidney disease (thank you, Emory University Hospital), cautioned us against dialysis, eventually explaining that due to all of Rhiannon's medical issues, the stress of dialysis would likely be worse than any benefit it would provide.

As she entered her twenties, Rhiannon began to experience chronic anemia, suffering dangerous drops in her blood counts, and began to rely on periodic transfusions just to keep going. These increased in frequency over the years, and if her counts dropped too rapidly, too quickly, she would end up spending several nights in the hospital as her team tried to get her numbers back up.

Friends, and then family, started to suggest that we needed to look into palliative care options, including hospice.

The hospital stays lasted longer and came more frequently. It started taking more units of blood to stabilize Rhiannon's counts. Finally, after Christmas one year she had a particularly difficult seven-day hospital stay in which she had to have a line inserted into her neck—her veins on her arms were beginning to scar because of all the bloodwork and transfusions she had endured over the years. She had to be sedated for both having the line inserted and removed. When she finally got home, just after New Year's, the three of us were exhausted and angst-ridden.

A few days later we met with Rhiannon's primary care physician, and the news was sobering. While her hemoglobin and platelet counts were barely acceptable (thanks to all the units of blood she had just received in the hospital), her kidney markers were elevated. It seemed that, despite Fran's vigilant efforts to manage every detail of Rhiannon's diet, her kidneys were still struggling, perhaps due to minerals like potassium and phosphorus present in the transfused blood. To address one of Rhiannon's problems meant exacerbating another. We mentioned hospice to the doctor, and she nodded. Her next words terrified us. "I think she only has a few weeks."

Fran reached out to Lisa, a dear friend who is a hospice nurse. The three of us had lunch and decided it was time to have a talk with Rhiannon. A few days later, Lisa and Liz, another good friend whose father recently had died after a good experience with hospice, came over to the house.

Because of the stroke, Rhiannon had the cognitive skills of only a ten-year-old, even though she was twenty-eight. So Lisa slowly and patiently explained to Rhiannon just what hospice was. This was a challenging moment, for Fran and I had carefully shielded Rhiannon from talk about being terminally ill—not because she didn't deserve to know, but because we wanted her approach to health care to be marked by hope. But it was time as a family to shift our emphasis from hope to trust.

The five of us sat down and Lisa took the lead, explaining to Rhiannon that the doctors had determined that no matter what they did, she was not going to "get better." Rhiannon took it in and asked her mom to hold her and cried for a minute or two—but only for a short time. Lisa continued, "You know, because of this, you have a choice. We can keep taking you to the hospital every time your blood counts drop, but we think you don't like going to the hospital. Is that right?"

"Bingo!" Rhiannon said, and we all laughed.

Lisa continued, "Rhiannon, there is a kind of health care called hospice. It is different from the care you get in the hospital. With hospice, we don't try to 'fix things,' but we do take good care of you. Best of all, you don't have to go to the hospital, unless *you* decide you want to. Do you think you would be interested in hospice?"

Rhiannon was silent for a moment, taking time to process this information. She looked at Lisa and said simply, "No more hospital?"

We were all wiping tears from our eyes. Lisa nodded. "No more hospital, unless you want it."

Rhiannon's next words haunted me. "I go to the hospital because my doctors want it." Even in her late twenties, the little girl who tugged at my beard the night we met still tended to form strong affectional bonds with people in her life, including her doctors, whom she treated as friends, not health care providers. In that moment it hit me: *Rhiannon has been cooperating with her grueling health care to please others; it's not what she necessarily wanted herself.*

"Well, you don't have to go anymore, if you choose hospice," Lisa pointed out.

"Yes," said Rhiannon, and so we began a new journey.

### Gifts and Grace

Fran went on family medical leave from her job at the school board, and I cancelled much of my own work, including delaying the two books I was working on and updating my blog infrequently.[2] We began an email newsletter to over one hundred family members and friends, announcing Rhiannon's and our decision. The response was swift and enormous. Over the next week, friends and family, some of whom we hadn't seen in ages, came by the house. My brother and sister-in-law drove up from Tampa; other relatives came from middle Georgia and South Carolina. Every day folks showed up, and Rhiannon reveled in the attention. The house felt like party central. As the weekend came near, it became obvious we would be spending it receiving, or dining, with a succession of loved ones.

I sat down with Rhiannon to review the schedule, feeling like her social secretary.

"This is the best week ever!" she declared. Long-suffering Rhiannon, for years she had been an extroverted prisoner living with two introverted parents. Now, finally, she was getting the social juice she loved. I shook my head bemusedly, hoping that I could be so at peace that when I enter hospice I also could have my "best week ever."

With the formal admission into hospice came its own flurry of activity. Since Rhiannon would continue to live at home with us, the care would come to our house. All her medicines were delivered to our front door, along with a succession of nurses, a social worker, and a chaplain. Fran and I took walks and talked about the enormity of the loss we were facing. We met with a priest, and a funeral home director, and got all the arrangements in order. After all, the doctor said it would just be a matter of weeks.

But Rhiannon, who had been beating the odds ever since she survived an eight-week stint in neonatal intensive care, was not ready to call it a day. Time passed, and by spring it became evident to us that her condition was not so much "declining" as more or less "stable." That's not to say there weren't signs of her illness progressing: she got tired much more easily, became very pale, and began using oxygen all night long, often sleeping for fourteen hours or more. By her twenty-ninth birthday in May, she began to show some hints of edema—swelling due to her failing kidneys.

Months into her hospice care, she remained in good spirits, always up for a visit with friends or another dose of her and my incessant banter. We settled into a new routine of pizza every Monday night at a local joint with a rotating array of close friends and good acquaintances, and on the night of her birthday we practically took the place over (when we asked Rhiannon what she wanted for her birthday, all she would say was "to spend time with friends").

Fran's sister-in-law suggested we read a book about hospice called *Final Gifts*; in reading that book I saw a reference to another, *The Grace in Dying*. That book begins with the author saying, "If you or your loved one is facing death soon, put the book down. And know that your loved one will be safe." At the time I read it, I wasn't sure just how soon Rhiannon's death would be. But I kept reading anyway, and I'm glad I did—for it talked about the spiritual dynamics of the dying process, approaching it through the lens of contemplation. It's a compelling (and I believe, liberating) way to view death and dying. I realized, both through my reading but especially through simply being with Rhiannon, that I was learning an entirely new way of approaching death.

It dawned on me that I was reaping the benefit of years of contemplative practice. Being affiliated with a monastery and seeing how accepting the monks are, in the presence of death, also proved a huge help. I'm not just talking about religious faith, although I believe a healthy faith in a loving and forgiving God certainly can be a blessing here. No, it's something larger than mere religion. It has to do with trust and love. It has to do with a recognition that unknowing, and silence, and even loss are not our enemies.

We began hospice convinced that Rhiannon would not make it to the beginning of spring. But as the weather turned warm, soon we stopped worrying about "how long she has." Friends began telling us stories of people who were in hospice for well over a year, so we decided it was just in God's hands.

Day by day, we simply lived with the contingency, the unknowing, and the necessity of remaining in the present moment. Fran went back to work, and I resumed working on my book about the silent spirituality of monks. In the summer, Fran had two months off from her job as a teacher's assistant. We took one final trip, to our favorite mountain getaway, Asheville. But Rhiannon's swelling was becoming more pronounced and transferring her became difficult. Back home, we started using a hydraulic lift to transfer her, and she began needing oxygen all day long.

Then, on a Tuesday night toward the end of August, Liz came over so Fran and I could have some respite, and we went to our favorite noodle joint and afterward took a night-time walk in the beautiful Virginia Highlands neighborhood of Atlanta. When we got home, Liz was crying. She told us that Rhiannon talked to her about dying.

Rhiannon never got out of bed after that. By the next morning we realized she was suffering and began giving her albuterol and small doses of morphine to alleviate her pain. Rhiannon stopped eating solid foods. Lisa said we could expect her passing by the weekend.

Early Thursday morning, just after midnight, Fran woke to find Rhiannon in considerable distress, gasping for breath, her lungs rattling. We called hospice, ended up with Lisa on the phone for over ninety minutes (we already knew she was an awesome nurse, but this sealed the deal) until the on-call nurse arrived at 2 a.m. It was a harrowing couple of hours, but finally we managed to get her breathing stabilized and get her calm to the point that she was resting (and Fran and I could get back to sleep as well).

We had been giving her a diuretic, but her kidneys simply stopped producing urine. She was on oxygen around the clock but required someone to monitor her continually because her nose would itch and she would push the oxygen mask away to scratch it. Then, without the oxygen, she would drop into lethargy until someone replaced the mask.

Our priest visited our home on Thursday and graced

Rhiannon with the Anointing of the Sick. For her *viaticum*—her final reception of Holy Communion— we shared one host among the three of us, Fran breaking a small piece and tenderly placing it in Rhiannon's mouth.

Over the course of her last few days, Rhiannon seemed almost to be moving in and out of her present life, at times speaking words that revealed she was deeply aware of what was going on, not only with herself but also her loved ones—and yet at other times clearly appearing to be lost in thought, or perhaps in prayer.

Saturday afternoon, Fran and the weekend nursing assistant were administering her medicine when they noticed her breathing abruptly changed. Her breaths came farther apart; the CNA took her blood pressure and found it was dangerously low. Fran called for me; I ran into the room to see Rhiannon totally unresponsive. I felt for a pulse and found it, weakly, but soon it was clear that she was letting go. Her eyes rolled back, her head drooped, and Fran embraced her, telling her she loved her and that if she needed to go, we understood. Rhiannon died in her arms.

### Simple as That

Before she died, Rhiannon asked Fran and me, individually, to promise her that we would care for the other.

Remember how I saw myself in Charlie Babbitt? As you may imagine, this weighed heavily on my heart for much of those final weeks. Joni Mitchell once sang, "You don't know what you've got until it's gone," but by God's grace I figured out what I was about to lose before Rhiannon passed. One day in January, shortly after she entered hospice care, I sat down with her and asked her if she would forgive me.

"What for?" she asked.

"Well, you know," I stammered. "For all the ways in which I wasn't a very good father."

"What do you mean?" she asked. She wasn't going to let me off easy.

It dawned on me that somehow I had managed to keep her in the dark about all the ways I resented the difficulties of long-term care. But of course, it did erupt from time to time, usually in terms of me losing my temper.

"Well, think of all the times I got mad at you and yelled at you."

"Oh, *that*," she said, with a laugh. "Yeah, that was no fun!"

"Well—I'm sorry."

"And I forgive you." Simple as that.

But I'm a slow learner, and so the week of Rhiannon's death, still feeling ashamed of my Babbitty ways, I came to her again, seeking some sort of absolution. "Rhiannon, I'm sorry . . ." I started.

She cut me off. "We've already had this conversation."

## Unteachable Lessons

The days following her death were a blur. At our pastor's urging, Fran and I left Atlanta to spend several days with friends in Asheville, leaving as soon as the funeral arrangements were made. It was a lovely respite, but we hit the ground running when we returned, putting together a slideshow for Rhiannon and writing our eulogies, or "words of reflection" as the priest called them. The vigil and funeral were, likewise, kind of a surreal kaleidoscope—hundreds of people at each event, with out-of-town family vying for attention with friends we hadn't seen in years. It was beautiful, wonderful—and for two introverts, exhausting. Rhiannon was the extrovert in our family—she would have just kept going, but Fran and I had to be mindful of our limits. We carefully designed the funeral to reflect music and readings that embodied Rhiannon's joyful, playful spirit. From the lyrical beauty of "All Creatures of Our God and King" and "Love Divine, All Loves Excelling" to the exuberance of an upbeat workout of "I'll Fly Away" (probably Rhiannon's favorite go-to-heaven song), every detail of the Mass was designed to emphasize celebration before mourning, joy before lamentation. Given who Rhiannon was, it was an easy liturgical feat to pull off.

Then, on the Monday after the funeral, Fran returned to work, and so did I—although for me that meant adjusting to a new sense of silence and emptiness that surrounded my home office since Rhiannon and her many nurses and caregivers were no longer there. I threw myself into my work, trying to find distraction from my grief rather than allowing it to overwhelm me. I figured I'd just as soon encourage the grief to come in waves over time, rather than all at once. I wasn't sure that was even possible, but it was my preference. As a strategy, it worked for about two months, and then I hit a wall. But maybe for those first two months, distracting myself was just what I needed.

What surprised me more than anything else was how *grateful* I felt in the midst of the grief. I knew enough about grief—and about how I grieve—to expect feelings of being overwhelmed, of sadness simply swallowing me whole, a sense of emptiness that seemed like it would never subside. Yeah, all of that rolled over me. But in the middle of it all, I just kept feeling wave after wave of appreciation, gratitude for the privilege of having been part of Rhiannon's life for over twenty-two years. For how much she taught me, about playfulness, about humor, about zest, about dignity in suffering, about letting life be imperfect, about forgiveness.

When I was working on the slideshow for Rhiannon's wake, I found a picture from her middle school years. At the time she was a cheerleader for the adapted sports program, supporting the wheelchair basketball team. She did this for two or three years; and each year she had a homecoming game with the usual half-time festivities. Twice, she asked me if I would escort her (and both times Fran, worried that I might not see how important this was to Rhiannon, spoke privately to me to make sure I would do it). This picture was from one of those years. I was smiling in the picture, but she was radiant. Such simple joy. I gazed into the picture and sobbed and sobbed.

I soon realized that all the talk about "stages of grief" was, at least for me, largely meaningless. Denial, anger, depression, bargaining, it all slammed me at once. I don't know how many days—certainly a few weeks, maybe longer, maybe even the first few months—I just kept walking around in a daze. I cried a lot, of course. I got sad. And then I also felt that luminous gratitude, for the amazing gift that my daughter was (is) to me and so many others, gratitude for how much I learned from her, gratitude for all the people who did and still love her and her mom and me.

Well-meaning friends and loved ones would say things like "At least she's in a better place now" or "She's no longer stuck in a wheelchair" or "Well, her suffering is over." That's all true and I believe it (thank heaven for my faith). I don't mean to criticize the genuine love and concern from the many people who cared. But every time I heard a comment like that I wanted to scream, "I'm not crying because I don't have faith or because I don't trust God. I'm crying because I miss my girl."

So maybe I still had a little bit of Charlie Babbitt in me, after all those years. Maybe, I suppose, grief has a self-involved quality about it. I don't think that's a bad thing. Because it all pointed to this: Rhiannon taught me more about living and love and spirituality and compassion than just about any person or any relationship I ever had—including Fran, including the monks and spiritual directors I've worked with, including the countless books I've read over the years. And one of the things I've learned from Rhiannon, and our journey together, was just how messy it all is. I was pretty much self-centered when I first met Rhiannon. And somewhere along the way, that diminutive girl, whose mind was compromised by a stroke and whose body was diminished by paralysis, taught me how to love.

I wish I could explain it. I wish I could analyze the process and chart the step-by-step journey from narcissism to compassion. But it isn't anything neat and tidy, and there's no making it tidy, either. To begin with, I wasn't *entirely* heartless, even at my Babbitty worst. And even during Rhiannon's final weeks, I was hardly cured of my narcissism, even if on most good days it seemed to be in remission. But there's no boiling this down to "Seven Steps to Learn Compassion" or "Action Plans for a Post-Selfish Life." The lessons I learned from Rhiannon are simply unteachable lessons.

It's been several years now since her passing, and I tell her (our) story from time to time. Almost at every telling, I meet someone who has a similar story to tell, of the unsung perseverance of caring for a sick child or grief that felt like gratitude or slowly discovering that love blossoms in our lives even when we're not expecting it. I've come to see that unteachable lessons are available to just about all of us—and I suspect that the more we need these unteachable lessons, the more likely they are to show up in our lives. Maybe they don't always entail suffering and loss, but I suspect they always involve some sort of deep interior transfiguration that is messy and unchartable and just can't be put into words. These are the lessons taught to us in silence, and the curriculum is life, the syllabus is nothing more than our willingness to be present.

# Feeling It in the Bones (or Not)

I want to tell you about an amazing moment in my life from back when I was a teenager.[1]

Before I do that, I want briefly to reflect on the irony of telling my story. I love telling stories, and I enjoy being a storyteller (not sure if I'm a good one or not, but I love the telling, and if someone else enjoys the hearing, that's a bonus).

Now, I tell *spiritual* stories, which means that I talk about God a lot. That kind of puts me at odds with one of the prevailing ideas in our society today: that it's better to *experience* God than to *talk about* God—or, worse yet, to listen to someone else talk about God (or read what they've written).

Therefore, as I tell this story, let me begin with a few disclaimers. This is just *my* story, nobody else's. I'm not suggesting that you should have, or try to have, an experience anything like mine. I believe every one of us gets called to a unique way of relating to God. You can't learn it from a book, and nobody can teach it to you. The only reason we should bother with someone else's spiritual story—whether we're talking about a great saint like Mother Teresa, a great mystic like Julian of Norwich, a renowned writer like Thomas Merton, or even just an ordinary person like me—is because every one of us has a unique story about God, and it's fun to read or hear other people's stories, even if ultimately it's better to discover our own God story.

Next, I think it's important to say up front that I was not, in any way, looking for what was about to happen to me. It was unasked for and unexpected.

Finally, please bear in mind that words cannot really convey what I am going to try to describe. Frankly, they get in the way, but when it comes to written communication, language is all we've got, so it'll have to do.

This amazing moment happened on a February evening not long after I turned sixteen. I was away from home for the weekend, participating in an event called "Winter Celebration" for high school students in the Virginia Synod of the Lutheran Church. I was not a particularly pious kid—my parents and I were active in our local church, and I did pretty much the normal things that kids my age did: I was an acolyte and attended Sunday school and participated in our youth group, what the pastor called the Luther League. But I was at least as interested in girls as I was in God, and actually a little bit scared of both. I'm an introvert, and back then it dominated my personality more than it does now: I basically was a dreamer who liked to read books and listen to "art rock" (bands like Yes and Pink Floyd) and so in social situations I tended to skulk in corners.

Winter Celebration took place at Massanetta Springs, a beautiful old Presbyterian conference center nestled in the Shenandoah Valley of Virginia. I had been to numerous events at Massanetta over the years and grew to love its stately, pre-Depression era charm. The center included a rambling old hotel with a large porch covered by rocking chairs, dozens of quaint cabins in the woods, and a grand amphitheater where outdoor church services were held, its musty classrooms filled with dusty Bibles and rings of chairs where teenagers would gather to discuss the meaning of life. I had been going to events at Massanetta since the seventh grade, and I loved it there. Each summer I spent a week there, canoeing on the lake, hiking on various woodland trails, browsing the bookstore where I first discovered the Chronicles of Narnia, or enjoying one of the best milkshakes in the world at the nearby snack bar. Even the springs themselves—producing water that was bottled and sold as a cure-all back in the Gilded Age—seemed sacred to me, almost like a North American version of an Irish Holy Well. For me, Massanetta Springs was what the Celtic Christians called a thin place, somewhere it's easier to recognize the nearness of God because the veil between the worlds is thin. The name Massanetta is partly derived from a Native American word meaning "a place of vision." On this particular weekend I would discover for myself just how apt that name is.

I had never before visited Massanetta in wintertime. The valley proved just as beautiful in February as in July, but it was an austere beauty, with a thin blanket of snow and a monastery-like silence. Unlike the summer programs, Winter Celebration took place mostly indoors, so rather than spending hours enjoying the surrounding natural beauty, the event focused more on community building through small group interaction and large gatherings for prayer and worship.

The high point of the weekend came Saturday night with a Communion service. All one hundred or so of the participants gathered for the informal Eucharist, driven by 1970s-style Christian folksongs (like "Kumbaya" and "We Are One in the Spirit"), with a couple of acoustic guitarists leading the singing as everyone held one another, arm in arm, swaying to the cadences of the music. I had participated in such informal worship services numerous times before, but this one seemed different from the start.

To begin with, I was moved by the sense of love in the room. A cynic might point out that we only had to put up with each other for a weekend before returning to our various homes throughout Virginia—but being cooped up in a church conference for an entire weekend would be enough to inspire plenty of antisocial behavior. Yet in this worshipful space, the harmony of our singing seemed to refract into a harmony of our souls. As I relaxed into a sense of connection with my fellow winter celebrants, I realized I was filled with a quiet joy and a serenity that seemed new to me, a feeling I had never registered before. This was not merely a fleeting moment of ecstasy—it was too grounded, too silent, too humble to be described as rapture. Not only that, it lingered, this mellow joy; it persisted for quite some time, perhaps several minutes, perhaps half an hour or more. Exactly how long I cannot say, for among other things I lost my sense of time.

Something shifted in my mind and in my heart, in my awareness and perception. Whatever it was, I could feel it in my bones.

This *amazing something* endured long enough to make a lasting imprint even in my bored adolescent mind. It astounded me, quite frankly. Indeed, the afterglow of this mysterious event remains with me to this day.

What, exactly, happened?

I suspect this will sound proud, arrogant, or pompous, and I don't want to come across as any of those things. But it's my very pride that keeps me from wanting to come across that way, so paradoxically, humility requires me to simply say what seemed to happen to me, as plainly as I can say. And the plainest I can put it is this: I felt as if I had suddenly recognized that I was one with God. I sensed that God was present, flowing in me and through me. Somehow—remember, I didn't *plan* on this and wasn't looking for it—I was perceiving or feeling or even knowing the intimate presence of God. I saw God, I felt God, I knew God's pulsating ubiquity within me—yet not just within me, rather within all things. God was fully, really, completely, mind-and-heart-expandingly *there*, in me but not only in me, indeed in everyone in that room. For a moment which may have lasted only a few seconds or a few minutes and yet seemed to open me up to the radiance of eternity, God touched me, God embraced me, God loved me, God flowed through me without condition, mediation, or separation.

It's that simple—but even though it really is that simple, it's also not so simple at all. These words on this page simply thud like rocks dropped on the ground; they totally fail to convey the energy and color, the resplendence and reverie, the silence and joy of that amazing threshold of initiation that changed me forever.

I call it a "moment," but it wasn't just a discrete point in time. This whatever-it-was lasted for a while. Don't ask me how long. Rationally speaking, I know by clock time it could only have been, at most, a few minutes. But in terms of heart time it seemed as if I had jumped off of the grinding succession of temporality into the endless nowness of eternity.

I sensed a spirit of unity, of oneness, of subtle, gentle love. I can't say "I became one with it" for there was no becoming, it just was.

As we sang and eventually shared the bread and wine of Holy Communion, it seemed to me as if the entire room began to glow. Not a physical shining, as if someone had turned on additional lights, but a radiance, a presence—words cannot describe this, they get in the way. Something changed in me, but outside me as well—slowly and subtly, but also suddenly and obviously, everything shimmered. Words fail. Every time I have tried to tell this story, I end up dancing with paradox to help me communicate what happened. Only words associated with light seem to capture the moment.

Shining.

Shimmering.

Glowing.

Luminous.

Resplendent.

Radiant.

Glimmering.

It's as if everything—the walls of the room, the various people within it, the bread and the wine being passed from hand to hand—sparkled with a light that I could still perceive even when I closed my eyes. Call it energy, perhaps, but even that word fails. While I perceived this as light, it also felt as if a new kind of love or joy had become manifest for the first time ever (or, at least, the first time ever in *my* life). I felt loved, loved like I never had before—and that's no insult to my family, for I came from a kind and caring home. It's just that what I found there that wintry evening took me somewhere I had never even imagined existed. To me it seemed as if every person in the room became radiant with a visibly miraculous glow.[2] Once I noticed it, I felt simply carried along by this deep peace and exultation I had never previously known.

It wasn't ecstasy, for I didn't feel like I left my body. Nor was it some sort of supernatural vision, for aside from the resplendence, physically things appeared just as they always had.

Some readers may wonder if this event had a chemical cause, but I was sober that evening. In fact, I can attest that later in my youth I did briefly experiment with entheogens like LSD or psilocybin—but those substances struck me as pale and physically jarring in comparison to the heart-expanding loveliness I had known that night.

Nor, to the best of my knowledge, was it any kind of psychological breakdown—it had no ill effect on me physically or emotionally, and the only lingering effect was that it left me with a sense of quiet contentment and a feeling of intimate, lasting connection to the God whom we worshiped that evening.

### After the Gift

This whatever-it-was was so gut-level real to me and so far beyond anything I might have imagined or tried to concoct that I actually thought something objectively miraculous had happened.

As best I could tell, this room in a Shenandoah Valley conference center had just witnessed some sort of profound moment in which God chose to reveal himself through light and love and ever-expanding joy. At first I assumed everyone must have seen and felt pretty much what I did.

Honestly.

It simply did not occur to me that this might have been just some sort of interior insight, granted to me alone. But I soon discovered to my surprise—and somewhat dismay—that others hadn't been aware of anything at all unusual that evening. After the service ended, I approached several friends and said, "Wasn't that *amazing*?" to which they responded with a totally noncommittal "Uh-huh."

Soon I realized that for some reason I had been given a unique gift. Suddenly feeling just a tiny pang of anxiety to accompany the lingering sense of union, I quickly excused myself and returned to my room, where for the rest of the evening I sat, alone and silent, and mulled over what had just happened.

### Looking for Words That Would Not Come

I wish I could say that, following that spiritual awakening that surprised me in my sixteenth year, I gracefully and gently adopted a life of prayer and service. But that's not what happened. If anything, my "mystical experience" (I feel uncomfortable using that language, but I don't know what else to call it) launched me onto a path marked by both shadows and light, by both peace and profound struggle, by searching for something I could not name, while sometimes remaining oblivious even when graces were staring me in my face. To put it bluntly, my spiritual life has been a mess. Which I know is not that different from many other people's spiritual lives. Mine just happens to be a mess with a big fat mystical awakening sitting in the middle of my adolescence.

I don't think that makes me unique or particularly special (and certainly not holy). A friend of mine who is a therapist and a Disciples of Christ minister assures me that adolescents quite often have some sort of moment of extraordinary awakening. Probably, like me, many of them find it difficult to talk about and maybe even a bit unsettling—even when it seemed suffused with light and felicity. I wouldn't be surprised if plenty of people have amazing moments like this, only to ignore them until they're forgotten—or at least tucked safely away in their subconscious, leaving nothing but a sense of longing for that which cannot be put into words.

Let me briefly share with you some of the consequences, both good and bad, of this singular evening that night in Virginia more than forty years ago.

It took me several more youth events (I attended two or three a year) before I realized, much to my chagrin, that God is not in the habit of throwing up a light show just because I wanted it. I went to whatever event I was attending, certain that *this time* I would be ushered into the presence of the mystery yet again. Then the big Communion service would happen, and . . . nothing. They were nice, very beautiful and enjoyable. But no awe-inspiring expansions of my heart, no palpable sense of everything suffused with love and light, no lingering vibration of energetic joy that would hum within me for weeks afterward. The first time I *didn't* have another mystical experience, I was crestfallen. Then after a few more youth events, I began to realize that an encore of Winter Celebration just wasn't going to happen, at least not for me.

It hadn't occurred to me that God could touch me in other ways, in other places. Remember, I'm a slow learner.

In the spring months after Winter Celebration, I threw myself into religion, reading the Bible cover to cover (I didn't understand much of it, but my enthusiasm kept me going) and ramping up my involvement in the church in various ways. We had a seminarian on staff that year, and she asked me if I had thought about seminary. It seemed the obvious choice: hadn't I been touched in a special way? So, I decided I had a call to ordained ministry (which, for a variety of reasons, never came to pass).

Still, all was not entirely sunny. I soon realized I didn't have anyone to talk to about this experience. I didn't know how to put it into words. You can see how challenging it is for me to talk about it after forty years of reflection—imagine how tongue-tied I felt after just forty days. I am not a particularly trusting person by nature (a topic we will return to later in this book), so I didn't feel comfortable struggling to articulate my experience with my parents, my pastors, or other adults in the church. Indeed, well over two years would pass before I finally stumbled across the kind of language that would help me to describe this singular moment in my life—when a friend gave me a book by Evelyn Underhill that introduced me to the language of Christian mysticism (I'll talk more about this later, too).

But before that happened, I discovered the dark side of spiritual experience.

### The Experience Trap

Six months or so after Winter Celebration, a new school year started, and I made some new friends, including a few folks who described themselves as charismatic Christians. They talked about things like speaking in tongues and being filled with the Holy Spirit. I had no idea what any of this meant, but I noticed that these kids talked about God as if God were really a part of their lives and not just some idea or abstract father-figure "up there." One of the guys and I started to hang out together, and he began to introduce me to Christian music, performed by artists like Phil Keaggy, Larry Norman, and 2nd Chapter of Acts. While it was not as intellectually stimulating as Yes or Pink Floyd, I responded to the devotional and worshipful tone of the music, and soon was listening to Jesus music almost as much as I listened to what my charismatic friends dismissively called "worldly music." To buy the Jesus music, I had to visit a Christian bookstore, where I also discovered books by writers like Dennis and Rita Bennett or Mike Warnke. A lot of the charismatic teens were reading Mike Warnke because his book was a lurid memoir about being a satanic high priest before coming to Christ. (Years later a major Christian magazine investigated Warnke's claims and found that there was no evidence he had ever been a satanist, but back then we took him at his word.) But it was the Bennetts' book *The Holy Spirit and You* that made the biggest impact on me. Based on several biblical passages that emphasize supernatural gifts or charisms that come from God through the Holy Spirit, it could have been subtitled *How You Can Become a Charismatic*. This spirit-filled way of being a Christian was, on the surface, a lot of fun—praising God with upbeat music, a heartfelt sense of devotion, and "singing in tongues," when believers joyfully and adoringly expressed their love for God through spontaneous prayers, sung in an "unknown language" that may have been of humans—or, it was said, of angels.

The more I learned about charismatic Christianity, the more it sounded a lot like what happened to me that previous February. And I wanted more of it. I began to go to charismatic prayer services twice a week—a non-denominational youth gathering on Saturday nights, and a Catholic-sponsored prayer service on Sunday afternoons. All while still going to the Lutheran Church with my mom and dad Sunday mornings.

Pretty soon I was following the step-by-step instructions in *The Holy Spirit and You* to pray for the baptism of the Holy Spirit—and the gift of speaking in tongues. As the Bennetts put it, "Now confess with your lips, but in the new language that the Lord is ready to give you. Open your mouth and show that you believe the Lord has baptized you in the Spirit by *beginning to speak*. Don't speak English, or any other language you know, for God can't guide you to speak in tongues if you are speaking in a language known to you. You can't speak two languages at once! Trust God to give you the words, just as Peter trusted Jesus to let him walk on the water. Speaking in tongues is a childlike act of faith."[3] One night in my bedroom, reading this book, I followed the instructions, and suddenly my prayer included several syllables that carried no meaning for me. There it was! I was speaking in tongues!

Dennis and Rita Bennett's book also introduced me to a new way of thinking about evil—and the devil. It suggested that the devil is a real sentient being who is actively trying to hurt people and uses all sorts of counterfeit spiritual experiences to cause harm in people's lives. In succession they condemned Buddhism, Hinduism, Islam, astrology, divination, ouija boards, spiritualism, hypnotism, witchcraft, hippies, and meditation. In essence, they insisted that spiritual experience is dangerous if it deviates in any way from their narrowly prescribed boundaries of what is acceptable to God. *The Holy Spirit and You* presents God as a patriarchal deity who must be obeyed—or else. This God rewards obedience, punishes disobedience, and brooks no compromise. This God frightens people into submission and is eager to send anyone to hell who doesn't conform to the spiritual experience of accepting Jesus as their personal Savior—and rejecting all other spiritualities.

For almost a year, I participated in the charismatic groups—one Protestant, one Catholic—as well as the Lutheran Church. I logged many hours of prayer and praise, dancing to joyful music, worshiping God in English and in tongues, singing sweetly my devotion to the Almighty. During this time I also participated in plenty of Bible studies and teaching sessions that always seemed to emphasize how dangerous the world outside of charismatic Christianity was. From yoga to zen, from Edgar Cayce to the Maharishi, from beer to sex, the message remained eerily consistent: that we lived in a scary, dangerous world, almost like Jim Carrey in *The Truman Show*. If we ventured off the "island" of safe charismatic Christianity, we were vulnerable to getting possessed or worse by the devil.

When my Lutheran pastor caught wind of what I was doing, he cautioned me that charismatic Christians placed more emphasis on their own experience than on God's grace. Meanwhile, I noticed that some of my Protestant charismatic friends disparagingly referred to Catholics as "dead Christians," while my Catholic charismatic friends dismissed Protestants as heretics.

I simply wanted to fall more deeply in love with God. But everywhere I turned, I kept running into Christians who kept attacking people who weren't just like them.

It all came to a head in the fall of my senior year in high school—some twenty-one months after my beautiful encounter with God at Massanetta—when I went to a weekend Catholic charismatic renewal conference in Atlantic City, NJ, with a group of my friends from the Sunday afternoon group I was attending. When we got to the conference, I was stunned to learn that the adults who brought all of us teenagers lied to the hotel about how many people were staying in the rooms. The youth were expected to sleep on the floor—which didn't particularly bother me (I was a teenager, after all), but the lying did. I brought it up with the man who was the leader of the community, and his response was blunt: "Go book your own room if you don't like it." I didn't have the money to do that, so I stayed put. But I was disillusioned and never went back to another charismatic prayer meeting after that.

Looking back to that time, I now realize that I was learning an unteachable lesson. An experience of God—especially one filled with pleasure and joy, like the sense of being baptized in the Holy Spirit—is like candy: it's sweet and delicious, but in itself it's not particularly nurturing. Looking back at *The Holy Spirit and You* after all these years, I can see how it promises a joyful and supernatural experience *of* God but overlays that on top of some pretty dicey ideas *about* God. What's the point of having a sweet experience of God if we *think* about God in terms of rewards and punishment or anger and control or needing to stay safe (and prove our worth) by rejecting anything that is deemed *counterfeit* or *impure*?

Ironically, in the years that followed my disillusionment with charismatic Christianity, I eventually explored pretty much everything that the Bennetts denounced as evil. I studied astrology and the writings of Edgar Cayce; I spent several years immersed in the worlds of paganism, Wicca, and goddess spirituality; I logged time as a hippie, chasing the Grateful Dead around the country, and I explored various techniques of meditation, including Eastern practices like shamatha and zazen, while also learning Christian practices such as centering prayer and the Jesus prayer. What did I find? Some of this stuff really did turn out to be dead ends (at least for me), but meditation in particular proved to be a rich and nurturing gift that brought me closer to God— not in terms of rewards and punishments, but by opening me to God's profound mercy, grace, and unconditional love.

My friend and fellow podcaster Kevin Johnson likes to talk about experience as a trap. His point is simple: when we get too caught up on the search for experience, we run the risk of making *an experience of God* more important to us than *God* is. And if we put all our emphasis on experience, we may end up confusing God, who we begin to see in very small ways, as merely the object of our experience, with ourselves as the all-important subject. (In the sentence "I experience God," the *I* becomes more important than *God*.) But there's still another danger that can emerge when our spirituality is focused on experience: if we just focus on feelings about God, without carefully reflecting on what we believe and why we believe it, then we run the risk not only of turning our experiences into idols, but our experiences can mask the fact that we carry within us some unhelpful, or even toxic, ways of thinking about God. Sooner or later, unhelpful or toxic images of God can undermine our faith, our happiness, and our ability to truly love and show mercy and forgiveness to others.

## How Does God Find You?

When a person has a powerful experience, one way to describe it is to say "I feel it in my bones!"

That night at Massanetta Springs, I felt in my bones how much God loved me—how much God is love—and how present God is in all our lives if only we could notice it. But I also felt in my bones the thrill of looking for *more* experiences of God, whether by trying to replicate the Massanetta experience at other youth camps or by coaching myself into speaking in tongues and then participating in communities that, I eventually learned, saw God in some unhelpful ways.

Now I'm left with a question that I think anyone who places too much emphasis on *experiencing* God rather than humbly *learning about the wisdom of God* needs to ask: It's all fine to feel God in our bones. But what if our bones don't know the whole story? Or, even worse, what if our bones lie? What if what we are feeling is *not* God but just our overactive imagination? What if it's just a projection of an idea about God? What do we do then?

How do we make sense of it when we discover that this God we have been experiencing turns out to be an angry jerk or a supersized control freak rather than a fountain of transforming love?

I'm not saying our experiences are necessarily counterfeit (like how the Bennetts dismissed meditation). But I think whenever we have an experience of God, we owe it to God (and to ourselves) to make sure that we're doing our homework and learning to discern the difference between merciful love and dualistic judgment, between anger that seeks to heal and anger that seeks to destroy, between a God who wants to promote community and relationships and who lavishly shares mercy and forgiveness with everyone, versus a very different kind of God who seeks to alienate people from one another by frightening his followers into submission and rejection of anyone who's different.

Experience may be important. But it's never enough.

The wise and wonderful mystic Julian of Norwich had an amazing experience of God. It lasted for about twenty-four hours. And then she spent twenty years praying on it and reflecting about it before finishing her one masterful book of mystical spirituality, *The Revelations of Divine Love*, also known as *Showings*. She had this to say about her experience:

"I am not good because of the revelation unless I love God better; and in as much as you love God better, it is meant more for you than for me. . . . For truly it was not revealed to me that God loved me better than the least soul who is in a state of grace, for I am sure there are many who never had a revelation or vision, but only the common teaching of Holy Church, who love God better than I do."[4]

Such sane wisdom here. An experience of God is never more than a means to an end, and the end is always more fully to know and respond to God's love in our lives. But we can reach that goal by ways *other* than experience. Julian points out that ordinary Christians, simply living a faithful life and learning the precepts of their faith, can be further along the path of love than she is, even with her dramatic experience of God. Likewise, if a person just reads about Julian's visions, and then becomes more truly God-loving than Julian is, the visions were meant more for that reader than for Julian herself.

May we all learn this lesson: to receive God in whatever way God may come to us, whether through an experience or through reading or through conversations with friends and mentors and loved ones, through ritual, through community, through service. It's all good.

What matters is not how you find God but rather how does God find you?

And may God find all of us luminous with hearts that love.

# The Page on Which
# the Words Are Written

So, here is how the story goes.

My parents took me to church, and at church I met David. David introduced me to Evelyn, who told me about Julian. Because of Julian, I learned about Shalem, and thanks to Shalem I discovered silence.

Let me unpack that a bit.

Like most middle-class Americans whose families still think religion is a good idea, I went to church for the first time when my parents took me. Ironically, it wasn't until I was in the sixth grade (which may have been a blessing, for precisely when most of my peers were getting sick of church, I still was fascinated by it). I was a shy kid (I believe I've already told you that once or twice), and I didn't always fit in with the other teenagers, whereas I did strike up a friendship with David, the hippie organist who looked like John Lennon circa 1969. David introduced me to jazz and cocaine and opium (fortunately I quickly figured out that hard drugs weren't for me, although I do still love jazz), but the most lasting contribution he made to my life was a small, garishly colored paperback book called *Mysticism* by Evelyn Underhill.

He gave it to me one Sunday afternoon, the summer before my freshman year in college. The previous night I had a scary dream in which the world was coming to an end. In the dream I panicked and scoured my room, trying to find a Bible, but all I could put my hands on was a copy of the Bhagavad Gita (it's been forty years and I still haven't figured out the meaning of that little detail).

When I told David about the dream, he went to his bookcase and handed me a copy of this book about mysticism. "I think you need to read this," he said. I never gave him the book back, and after I went to college we didn't see each other for over thirty years. I finally reunited with him one day when I was back in my hometown for my father's funeral. I apologized to him for never getting his book back to him, but he said, "Oh, I gave several copies of that book away, back in the day. It was meant for you."

I know it's a cliché to say it, but Evelyn Underhill's *Mysticism* changed my life. Not only did it set into motion the chain of events that I am about to describe to you, but it also has been the direct inspiration of several books I've written. It's the book that finally helped me to be able to think about, and talk about, my initiation into the mystery that night at Massanetta Springs. It provided my first introduction to many of the great mystics of the Christian tradition. I suppose I would have learned about Julian of Norwich sooner or later without reading Underhill, but it was through Underhill that I first met Julian, so Evelyn gets the credit.

Fast forward almost five years to my last year in graduate school. One Sunday morning I was hanging out with my girlfriend who was reading the *Washington Post*; she looked up at me and said, "There's going to be a play at the Cathedral about one of those mystics you like." God bless her for her eagle eye—she saw that the National Cathedral was sponsoring a one-woman play about Julian of Norwich, which would take place on May 8 (which is one of two possible days when Julian had her visions[1]). The play, *Julian*, dramatized her life, drawing from her theology and even her ministry as a spiritual director, alluding to her relationship with another medieval mystic, Margery Kempe.

I called the Cathedral and learned that tickets were free, but I should get them in advance. On the Saturday before the play, I went into town—no easy feat in those days, as I had no car; I had to catch a bus from my home in suburban Fairfax, VA, to Arlington, where I caught the metro to the Cleveland Park Station before walking a mile to the Cathedral. Fortunately, it was a glorious spring day, and there was some sort of gardening or flower festival taking place on the Cathedral close, so the atmosphere was truly festive as I walked up, found the tickets (in the gift shop I believe, where I probably spent too much money on books), and proceeded to fall in love with that grand twentieth-century neo-Gothic edifice.

Back at the Cathedral the following Tuesday—the evening of the eighth—I joined a small but appreciative audience in the "Great Choir" (nave) of the Cathedral, where we were treated to a short concert of medieval music before the actress Roberta Nobleman took the stage. As she delivered her performance, based much on Julian's own words, in fourteenth century dress there in a dark cathedral nave, a sense of timelessness washed over me, and I felt caught up in the wonder of Lady Julian's visions—even though I had not yet read her book for myself.

After the play, I noticed a table set up behind the audience, where an organization called the Shalem Institute was handing out information. Shalem was one of the co-sponsors of the evening's play. I chatted with the woman at the table, who informed me that they would be hosting a "Julian of Norwich Quiet Day" the following Saturday. Right there on the spot I registered for the event and wrote a check for the registration fee. Years later I came across the cancelled check; in the memo line I wrote "Julian Seminar." Clearly, I had the mind of a graduate student—and had no idea what a quiet day was.

But I found out. I went to Cleveland Park Congregational Church that next Saturday, where thirty or so folks convened to share a day of silence, prayer, and reflection organized around the words and wisdom of Lady Julian.

After each of several brief talks on this or that aspect of Julian's teachings, we had anywhere from thirty to sixty minutes of time for silent prayer and reflection. I had never experienced communal silence before.

I often hear people say that they are uncomfortable with silence, they're afraid of it, they don't know what to do with it. I must be a lucky man—for when I first encountered intentional silence in a communal setting, on that spring day in 1984, I took to it like a duck to water, pardon the cliché. My immediate emotional response to having forty-five minutes of silence with other people was a quiet but joyful sense of "so *this* is what I've been looking for." I don't want to over-romanticize that day—or my relationship with silence in the years that followed; I've certainly logged many moments in silence that have been restless, distracted, or anxious. But that initial encounter was, for me, an opening up: a gateway into a new and larger world. It was a moment of coming home and recognizing who I truly am.

### Relating to Silence

In telling this story (especially by beginning with Mom and Dad), I suppose I might just be reflecting on how important relationships are to us, for even our earliest bonds (like those with our parents) can set into motion life-changing connections, loves, and opportunities. I suppose all of us have multiple chains of relationships that shaped our lives in meaningful and surprising ways. For example, I could also talk about how my high school friend Dennis told me to read a book called *The Spiral Dance*, which introduced me to the neo-pagan movement, and then, years later, at a neo-pagan gathering I met my friends Logan and Danae, who in turn invited me to a festival they were hosting, where I met my wife. See how it works?

But for now I want to focus specifically on silence. Because, interestingly enough, I think we human beings can have a relationship with silence, just like we have a relationship with our spouse or God or our best friend or a book that changed our life.

I may have fallen in love with silence on that spring day at the Shalem quiet day, but of course it wasn't my first encounter with silence. As best I can remember, as a child or teen I never thought of silence as something to be cherished or enjoyed for its own sake. Silence was that awkward thing that happened when I tried to talk to a girl who I thought was so cute and I could never be good enough for her, so of course the words wouldn't flow, and I stood there tongue-tied until my face flushed with embarrassment, and she figured out I wasn't very self-confident, which is a major buzzkill and pretty much ended any chance I had with her (alas, this happened more than once). Even at church, if we were instructed to pray silently, the idea was that no one was speaking out loud, but in my head I was chatting up a storm to God.

Therefore, the Julian of Norwich quiet day was a watershed moment for me, and while I had not yet made the connection in my mind that silence had something essential to do with spirituality and mysticism, when I found out how beautiful and attractive silence in a group setting was, I was hooked.

Shortly after that quiet day, I began to work with my first spiritual director through Shalem, a grandmotherly woman named Lin who was quite patient with this shy, nervous twenty-something; she patiently instructed me on the techniques of meditative prayer and insisted that if I was as serious about spirituality as I said I was, I would make it a daily priority. Eventually, I participated in a couple of programs through Shalem to help deepen my own contemplative practice and to give me some basic insights into leading contemplative prayer groups. I wish I could say that it was the beginning of a beautiful relationship (with silence, that is). But alas, silence and I have had about as rocky a love affair as you could imagine.

To begin with, I discovered that silence is *shy*—even shyer than I am. I would sit down for twenty minutes of meditative prayer, eager to bask in the silence, only to find that I had an internal dialogue going on that simply refused to shut up. Compared to the booming, stentorian monologue of my mind, silence was the retiring wallflower who simply sat in the back where no one would notice her.[2] Eventually I realized that even if I was "trying to find God" or, worse yet, "trying to experience God," that *searching* was in itself a departure from silence: it was as if even my subconscious was noisy to the extent that I tried to manage or control my experience during contemplative or meditative prayer.

Over the years, silence and I would get close and then drift apart. I would spend many days—sometimes months or even years—allowing dust to settle on the meditation cushion I purchased from a Buddhist mail-order company so I could "sit" just like we did at Shalem. But then I would read an inspirational book or visit a monastery or have a particularly meaningful conversation with a spiritual director, and I would wipe the dust off of the cushion and take a seat. And so it went, even during the seasons when I wandered away from Christianity and explored neo-paganism. Then, when I traded in paganism for Catholicism, silence (and silent forms of praying) became more important to me than ever.

There were many reasons why I became a Catholic after my time away from Christianity (rather than just returning to the Lutheran or the Episcopal Churches), but one of the big reasons was my attraction to the spirituality of Trappist monks, who had a monastery just a half hour's drive from my home. When I began to hang out with the Trappists, suddenly silence had a bigger presence in my life. She still seemed to be pretty shy, especially on the inside, but as I began to study with the Lay Cistercians (the community of laypersons who formally receive spiritual guidance from the monks), I began to get to know silence a little bit better. And it wasn't just a Catholic or a Trappist thing, either—around this same time I also began to occasionally take classes at the local Shambhala Meditation Center, where I was introduced to meditation in a Tibetan Buddhist way. As I began to recognize silence in my life more and more, one day I had a pretty sizable insight.

Silence was always there.

In other words, even when my inner voice was chatting away as loud as can be, it's not as if silence had left the building (or left me). Rather, silence simply hung out in the background while I kept distracting myself with whatever hit song I was humming to myself or whatever argument I was having with this or that coworker, or whatever other idea or feeling or story line I kept repeating within.

In his book *A Brief History of Everything*, integral philosopher Ken Wilber maps out the various stages or levels of human consciousness, beginning with infants and moving through the ordinary dynamics of growth and developing and progressing onward to nonordinary or mystical dimensions of consciousness, including what he calls "psychic," "subtle," "causal," and "nondual" awareness. Each of these stages represents a higher/deeper unfolding of knowing, seeing, feeling, intuiting, and comprehending—you could say that each one is a rung on the ladder leading to God. But the final stage, the nondual, is what mystics would call the unitive life: union or communion with God. It's where you go when you've climbed up and off the ladder. As Wilber describes it, "The paper on which the diagram is written is the 'highest' stage, which is not really a stage at all but the nondual Ground of the whole display. Spirit is both the highest level—'causal'—and the Ground of all levels—'nondual.'"[3]

Silence is the paper on which the ink of human consciousness is printed. All our thoughts, our feelings, our emotions, our imaginations and daydreams, our compulsions, our primal urges—it's all ink on the paper.

Silence is the paper. Silence is the screen on which the film of our lives is projected. And silence, more than anything else within us, is the doorway to the presence of God.

Some Christians might get a bit squeamish when I talk about finding God within. Isn't that the kind of rhetoric that new agers and neo-pagans indulge in? When we talk about "God within," aren't we flirting with (gasp) pantheism?

But it's quite biblical to talk about God within us. We may have all grown up in churches that do a fine job of ignoring the solid Christian teaching that God is found within—but it's there in black-and-white if we simply will look for it. "God's love has been poured out into our hearts through the Holy Spirit, who has been given to us," says no less an authority than Saint Paul, in the letter to the

Romans (5:5). And before you go trying to tell me that there's a difference between God's love and God, keep in mind that Scripture bluntly tells us "God is love," going on to note that those who live in love, live in God—and God lives in them (1 John 4:16). Which brings us to the words of Jesus himself: "Abide in me as I abide in you" (John 15:4), which is as good as saying that our calling is to remain not only in Christ but truly in God, and God in us—for Jesus clearly taught that he is one with God (John 10:30).

God is one with Christ, and Christ abides in us. God has poured God's love into our hearts through the Holy Spirit (and our bodies, incidentally, are temples of the Holy Spirit—see 1 Corinthians 6:19, which comes just two verses after Saint Paul says that whoever is united with Christ is one with him in the Spirit).

So God is found within—and the doorway to God's throne in our hearts is the silence on which all of our awareness is minted.

According to the Trappist monk Thomas Keating, "Silence is God's first language; everything else is a poor translation. In order to hear that language, we must learn to be still and to rest in God."[4] Likewise, Rabbi Rami Shapiro notes that "the deepest language of the soul is silence."[5] Put those two together and do the math. Silence is God's first language, and silence is the deepest language of *our* souls. Therefore, silence is the medium by which we communicate with God.

Look at one of the most powerful images of God in the Old Testament: 1 Kings 19:11-12, when Elijah is on the mountain of the Lord, waiting for God's presence. It's a dramatic story, for first there is a mighty wind, but God is not in the wind; then there is an earthquake, but God is not in the earthquake; and then a fire, but God is not there either. After this elemental stripping away of mighty forces that are *not* God, what does Elijah encounter? The Hebrew words are *qôl dəmāmâ daqqâ*—which gets translated as "a still small voice" (KJV), or "a light silent sound" (NAB), or "the sound of sheer silence" (NRSV). We encounter God in and through the voice of silence.

If we write a letter to someone, we use pen and ink. An email requires electricity and a tablet or similar device. Even talking to someone requires air to carry the vibrations of our sound and a quiet enough environment that the listener can hear what is said. All communication requires a means for the connection to take place. In the mystical life, we need silence to communicate with God. And God needs silence to communicate with us.

Right away I can think of a few good folks I know through social media who will immediately object, "But what about the Word?" By which they mean the Bible (or, for that matter, Christ, the Word of God). It's not either-or. Sacred Scripture is a beautiful means by which God communicates to us. As you can see, I quote it plenty myself. But if we take the Bible at its word, we know that God wants to do more than just send us a memo through this collection of ancient writings. God wants to be present in our hearts—or, perhaps better said, God *is* present in our hearts and wants us to notice.

The means by which we notice God's immediate presence in our lives? Silence.

### Deep Listening

This insight, that silence is always there and it's a way we encounter God, really is nothing special. For me it wasn't new information so much as a new noticing. I first read Ken Wilber's book in the 1990s and had been familiar with Thomas Keating for almost as long and of course the New Testament even longer. But as I began to pay more attention to the silence that was always there, always inside me, I realized that as important as it was for me to learn what other people had to say about silence, ultimately I had to discover it for myself. I had to *be* silent. I had to pay attention. I had to listen to the silence within me. Which meant being patient with my interior monologue, gently allowing it to slow down long enough so that I could notice the silence between the words.

In other words, all the reading, all the Bible study, all the *lectio divina*[6] that I had done over the years ultimately only mattered to the extent that it encouraged me to sit down, shut up, and see (and hear) for myself.

Incidentally, I think this is the root of *obedience*, a terrible word that has come to mean some pretty distasteful things in our culture, far different from what I think ancient spiritual masters like Saint Benedict meant when they used the word. We equate obedience with a submissive following the rules, seeing it entirely in terms of dominance and compliance, and then speculating about what happens when one is asked to obey something wrong (like a Nazi being ordered to gas the Jews and other inmates in a concentration camp). But that kind of submissive compliance is not authentic obedience at all; in fact it's pretty much the opposite of true obedience. The word *obedience* is related to *listening* (compare *obedience* with *audience*). True obedience emerges out of that silence deep within us where we listen for the still, small voice of God, the light silent sound, the sound of sheer silence.

Silence is not an absence; silence is a presence. We need light to see someone we love, and we need silence to listen for the wordless voice of God deep within. This is not easy in our world, for we have many noisemakers to distract us from silence. Music, television, the Internet, our various electronic devices—not to mention the industrial sounds that invade our lives, from engines and airplanes to even the quieter but omnipresent hums of air conditioners, refrigerators, and other appliances. When my daughter was dying, the hiss of her oxygen machine became the soundtrack of our lives.

Many have discovered that it is necessary to take refuge in monasteries or meditation centers or simply deep in the forest to withdraw from all the external sources of noise, just to find a chance to sort through all the internal noise to discover the shy silence deep within. To do that, we might find that we also need a skill like centering prayer or mindfulness meditation. The chief result of clearing away *external* noise is simply to allow us to come face to face with all the *internal* noise. So often we discover the paper only to realize how covered over it is with ink.

But we learn to sit with it. And over time we recognize that the paper is always there: we couldn't see the ink without it. We can't listen to the endless noises in our lives without the silence that conveys the noise to us. Ultimately, our task is to be present to the silence *even within the noise*. I know an elderly monk who says, after many decades of cloistered life, "I no longer pay attention to silence; now I simply *am* silence." I think he's on to something. And I know him well enough to know that he has a noisy brain just like the rest of us. But he also has learned to listen beneath the noise and between the words to the point where silence is no longer an object of his listening but rather is the subject of his life.

In his book *Into the Silent Land*, Martin Laird describes three doorways that lead to ever-deeper contemplative prayer. Each doorway simply takes us deeper into the silence that is already present within us. It's well worth reading. But even as I write these words, I am humbled by the recognition that no teacher can ever initiate us into the mysteries of silence. We all must take that journey for ourselves. If you're a slow learner like me, it will likely take years if not decades—all the more reason to get started today. When you listen to the silence, you will listen to many other things: your own boredom, your own restlessness, your own judgmentalism ("this is a waste of time!"), perhaps even your own anxiety or your own ego-driven desire to have a special experience of God.

All of this is simply ink on the page.

Again and again and again, we are invited to return our obedience—our deep listening—away from the words and feelings that our ego keeps serving us, back into the abyss of pure silence. Again and again and again, we are invited to lift our eyes away from the ink and back to the page on which the words are written. And at a level deeper than our conscious awareness, God speaks to us. Listen.

# That Word, "I Do Not Think It Means What You Think It Means"

"You are just too stuck in your head."

I've heard that a lot over the years. Mostly from my friends, people who presumably had some firsthand knowledge of how cranially impacted I really was—and who cared enough about me to try to get me to change, hopefully for the better. I don't hear it as much anymore. I don't know if that means nowadays I'm *less* stuck in my head or simply that my friends have given up trying to get me to change. For that matter, maybe it just shows that I've become more careful in picking friends who don't care if I'm stuck in my head or not.

But there were times in my life when more than just one or two friends would tell me this. And looking back, I have to admit that I think they were right.

I really was stuck in my head.

Not literally, of course, as if my body had somehow gotten scrunched up into my skull (eww, that's a scary thought). But figuratively, which is to say I was someone who relied more on logic than on emotions, more on my intellect than my intuition, more on ideas and reason and science rather than simply trusting my feelings, my dreams, or even the inarticulate wisdom of my body, to navigate my way through life.

I'm trying to recall the first time someone told me this. I don't remember who it was or when it was, although I think I was in college. But what I do remember is being dumbfounded by this observation. I honestly had no idea what my friend meant. Which, I suppose, goes to show how right they were. It was inconceivable to me that there could be a way of managing your life *other* than relying on facts, data, and thinking things through. Just as I don't recall the where and the when, I'm drawing a blank trying to remember what the context was (i.e., what I said or did that merited this observation). I think it was a girlfriend who first said this to me; she probably was pretty exasperated at how clueless I was over whatever it was. Ah, the circumstances are lost in the cloud of forgetting. Which I suppose is just as well. I remember the phrase itself, though. I remember feeling confused, and I think I said in reply, "What does *that* mean?" Which, if my memory serves me at all, led pretty much to the end of the conversation.

But I would hear it again—and again. Until I finally got some glimmer as to what this meant (and what to do about it).

## Sherlock, Spock, and Sheldon

When I was a kid, my heroes were Mr. Spock, Tom Swift, Danny Dunn, and Brains Benton. People below a certain age may not be familiar with all these literary eggheads— but in their day, they were all notable for their expansive intellect and cool, emotionally detached approach to life and to solving problems. Tom, Danny, and Brains in particular made great characters for tweenage mystery and science-fiction novels aimed at boys, but I shudder to think what these characters would have been like had they really existed (and grown up) in real life—think Sheldon Cooper meets Benedict Cumberbatch's Sherlock Holmes, and you begin to get the idea.

The only problem: all these nerd icons, from Spock to Sheldon, compensate for their emotional ineptitude by being geniuses. No such luck for me. I was as clueless as them all, but not nearly as smart as any of them, more's the pity.

I was always a rather socially awkward kid, the kind who got picked last for the team sports and who never even got close to winning the President's Physical Fitness Award. But I loved to read and had some decent math skills, so I tended to be my best when it came to book learning. You can see where this would lead: as I progressed through my public school years, I naturally put my energy into the areas where I was more likely to succeed (or at least get a decent grade). By the time I figured out that being one of the cool kids (to say nothing of impressing the girls) had more to do with being well-rounded than with being a bookworm, it was too late. My destiny lay before me, and a wormy destiny it was.

Soon the time came for me to go to college, where my friends started pointing out to me my stuck-in-the-headedness. By then I lacked the capacity to see how limited (and limiting) my Spock-revering mind really was. I was blind to how my idolatry of logic actually kept me from being a more trusting person or a more empathic friend or more willing to simply follow my heart and make decisions based on what would make me happy, rather than what I had decided was "the most rational."

Granted, on occasion making the most reasonable choice really did make me happy. But sometimes there really was a disconnect between my feelings and my thinking. When that happened, relying only on my narrow notion of logic, I had no idea how to navigate the difference, so I basically got stuck.

Stuck in my head: see?

Even an ordinary teenage rite of passage—say, asking a girl to go to a dance—flummoxed me beyond all hope. From the vantage point of midlife, I now understand that even the popular kids are not immune from the angst of adolescence and have to overcome the jitters in all sorts of social situations. But at the time, having a sense of solidarity with all the other angst-ridden teenagers simply was not on my radar. For me, being so reliant on my cleverness to navigate my way through school, bumping up against something where book smarts couldn't get me to where I wanted to go left me, well, flummoxed.

I remember so clearly the first time I set out to invite a girl to a dance. I was in junior high school, and since I was utterly terrified of actually asking her out in person, I figured the "logical" thing to do was to call her up. I managed to get her phone number (how I pulled that off, I have no recollection) and sat down one Saturday afternoon to ring her up and ask her out. And then I noticed something unusual: my heart began to pound. My hands began to sweat. That was *really* unusual. And that led to my breathing becoming shallow. Then my fingers began to feel numb.

At this point, completing a simple task like dialing the phone was out of the question. I was doing my best simply to remain alive.

I can look back at this, or other, inglorious moments of my youth and feel plenty of compassion for my younger self. Somehow, I never got the memo that feeling nervous and feeling excited resulted in similar physiological changes in my body. At the time, however, I assumed the worst—that the mere thought of asking a girl to the dance was enough to induce a simultaneous stroke, heart attack, and nervous breakdown. I had no way of knowing just how normal my feelings were. (Remember, I hadn't quite figured out that I *had* feelings, let alone was capable of interpreting them well.) Nevertheless, I was clever enough to recognize that my body was doing things I had no conscious control over, but I lacked the smarts—street smarts or otherwise—to just "feel the fear and do it anyway," as a revelatory self-help book I would read in my thirties would explain to me.

Looking back, I'm really glad I came of age in the 1970s, when traditional gender roles were beginning to break down. My first steady girlfriend was a take-charge type who pretty much made all the moves. If I had never met her or had been born twenty years earlier, I might have ended up becoming a monk (not that that's a bad thing, but I don't think it really was the path meant for me).

Thank heaven, I eventually did figure out how to communicate with girls (and later, women) enough to have a few romances along the way, and eventually marry a wonderful life partner. But thanks to 20/20 hindsight, now I can ruefully see that I was a fairly limited boyfriend—"with the personality of an artichoke," as one friend of mine wryly observed. Not because I didn't like the people I dated, but because I was—well, you know—more robot than Romeo.

### Getting Unstuck

What I'm about to say may be obvious to most people, but it was a revelation to a slow learner like me. One day my college sweetheart and I were in a grocery store, and some minor altercation took place between us—something on the level of, she wanted to buy wine but I wanted beer. And I got furious. She was kind enough to let me act like a spoiled brat for a few moments, but as soon as I calmed down she said, "You're not just angry about the Heineken. Something else is going on here." As we talked it through, I slowly began to realize that I didn't have the first clue how to express being annoyed or irritated in an appropriate way.

If something annoyed me, I would do *anything* but talk about it. Then something else would irritate me, and so I stuffed those feelings as well; the process repeated itself a few more times, and then one day something really little and minor would set me off, and suddenly I was swearing in the middle of the food store—all because my girlfriend said, "I don't want beer" or something equally minor.

I also clearly remember the first time someone—that same girlfriend, actually—said to me, "It really is okay to want to be happy. And to do what it takes to be happy." I was dumbfounded, not so much that she believed that, but that being happy was nowhere on *my* map of how to navigate through life.

As I write these words, even I can see how obvious it was that I spent too much time stuck in my head. Which means not only that I couldn't figure out what to do with *good* feelings (like love or sexual attraction), but I certainly had no idea how to manage *difficult* feelings (like anger or jealousy or feeling left out).

The more I discovered how important something like *emotional intelligence* really is, the more I realized that my devotion to Mr. Spock and his ilk left me unprepared to deal with even the fairly basic challenges in life and love and relationships.

Thankfully, over the years and because of some really patient, caring friends along with a few wonderful spiritual directors and therapists, I slowly learned to recognize that there really is this something called a "body" dangling beneath my head, and that it has feelings and desires and needs, and that life really is better when I pay attention to it and try to take good care of it.

I'm not suggesting that feelings are *more* important than logic or reason. Not hardly. If that were true, think of the implications. For starters, the average romantic relationship might never last more than a few weeks (or days or minutes)—however long it would take for one member of the couple to feel turned on by someone else. Thankfully, most of us have learned that romantic attraction is a fickle thing whereas true love is a commitment, and we have found a way to balance what we feel with what we think.

But the long, slow journey out of being stuck in my head, and toward learning about the needs and language of my heart, meant letting go of a lot of ideas that I had uncritically accepted as a kid. Like thinking science is better than art. That logic is more reliable than poetry. That reason always trumps intuition when it comes to making decisions. That feelings, ultimately, aren't that important.

My problem was not that I loved my mind. My problem was that in doing so, I learned to ignore, and perhaps even denigrate, my body.

As human beings, we acquire knowledge through thinking—through the application of logic and reason—but we also rely on our senses, and our "body knowledge"—our intuition, our feelings—to learn and to know. Call that two ways of knowing: the thinking approach and the feeling or embodied approach. The main thing I had to unlearn was this idea that one way of knowing is *better* than the other. Head knowledge is not superior to embodied knowledge—but neither is the opposite. For me to get cranially *un*stuck did not require replacing logic with intuition or throwing common sense out of the window in favor of emotional impulses. Rather, it meant learning to partner my head and my heart. To allow my thinking mind and my feeling heart to communicate with one another. And to give myself the patience to take the time to sort it all out. (I'm an introvert, and this means that sometimes it takes time, lots of time, for my head and my heart to figure each other out. Well, so be it.)

Even though it's been years now since the last time someone accused me of being stuck in my head, I cannot claim to be a master of how to balance my head and my heart, how to integrate thinking and feeling into my self-knowledge or communication skills. But just like a lot of people will joke about being a "recovering Catholic" or a "recovering workaholic"—well, I'm a recovering Vulcan. And like anyone else in recovery, I've slowly learned that even the awkwardness and obstacles of being in recovery sure beats the limitations that I lived with beforehand.

## The Body and Mind of Christ

The New Testament tells Christians that we are "the body of Christ" (1 Corinthians 12:27), but also that we "have the mind of Christ" (1 Corinthians 2:16). I don't know if Saint Paul intended this or not, but it seems to me that we need *both*—both the body and the mind of Christ. We need his head and his heart. If we want a healthy and holistic relationship with Christ—and with each other—we need the discernment of his mind as well as the wisdom of his body.

Earlier I talked about how it can be a mistake if we overemphasize *experience* as a way of approaching spirituality. Not that there's anything wrong with experience, but a healthy spiritual experience needs to be embedded in a thoughtful approach to God. In other words, part of having a healthy experience of God is learning to carefully think about God in wise and good ways. So now we come to the other part of this equation. If we allow our faith to get stuck in the head, we run the risk of letting doctrine and dogma be all that matters to us, faithwise. That would mean ignoring the many quiet but real leadings and longings of our hearts. That leads to its own flavor of trouble.

Every now and then, somebody stumbles across my blog about contemplative prayer and spirituality, which is interfaith friendly but written from a Christian perspective—and they leave a lengthy comment that essentially entails a detailed argument as to why the writer doesn't believe in God. Or doesn't like Christian mysticism. Or thinks Catholicism is a departure from biblical truth. The point of the argument varies from writer to writer, but the structure of the comment follows an all-too familiar pattern. The writer simply musters a lot of evidence and a lot of logic to support his point of view (or her viewpoint, although it usually seems to be men who write like this). Over the years I have slowly learned that it is best to ignore comments from folks like this. They want a debate—and they only want to talk in terms of their own logical propositions.

For some reason, being stuck in the head seems to lead a certain type of person to want to debate. I know this is true because even though I'm a recovering Vulcan, I still feel tempted to join in the debate whenever someone dangles the bait in front of me. It must be the same impulse that makes some chess players so aggressive.

Repeatedly, I have to stop and listen to my heart, and my heart always says, "What will you achieve by arguing with this person? Nothing. You're not going to change his mind, and he's not going to change yours. The argument is just a big ego trip to see who is the cleverest or can amass the most facts or can quote the most Bible verses or cite the most philosophers."

When I stop to truly listen to my heart, I know better than to stroke my ego in this way. But even now, after years of being a recovering Vulcan, I still don't always listen to my heart.

Not long ago I got a blog posting like this from an atheist. He was offended by the fact that God doesn't heal amputees.[1] He insisted that because Jesus promised to grant the requests of two or more Christians who pray for the same things, but that there has never been a documented miraculous healing of an amputee, that it proves God doesn't exist.

It was quite a lengthy, detailed post. The writer set out his argument in careful and great detail.

I read through it and decided (against my better judgment) to reply. I suggested that his argument is based on a literalistic reading of the Bible, but not all Christians read the Bible that way. Furthermore, I said that I was more interested in people who were actively helping others (including, we may assume, helping amputees) than in people who just want to debate topics like "Does God exist?" or "Is prayer effective?" And, thinking I was being friendly, I suggested that if his lack of faith in God resulted in his being a kinder, more caring, and more compassionate person, then that was good enough for me since I believed that faith ultimately is more about love than about having all the right answers.

The next day, this guy posted a comment that was even longer than his first one. He dismissed my suggestion that love was what really mattered and went back to insisting that Christianity is a false religion because it fails to live up to his idea of what is (or is not) scientifically credible.

At that point I decided to ignore the guy. But that old part of myself that wants to be the precocious child of Sheldon Cooper and Hermione Granger really wanted to keep stoking the argument. Then I began to listen to my heart, and my heart said no. And as I sat and reflected on where my heart was leading me, I got this insight: you can argue for (or against) proofs of God's existence, but no one will ever definitively prove the other side wrong. The argument just keeps going. It's basically a trap, and what gets trapped? The ego.

It reminds me of C. S. Lewis's wickedly acerbic description of a theology club in hell. They meet once a week to deliver papers and debate on all the important theological issues of the day. But they're in hell! They're so busy debating about God that no one in the club has ever bothered to actually *relate* to God—to respond to the call of divine love in their lives.

We need both the mind and the body of Christ. Yes, we need careful reason and mature logic and a well-formed intellect. But we also need a heart that has learned how to love.

## "Inconceivable!"

In the movie *The Princess Bride*, one of the bad guys, Vizzini, likes to use the word *inconceivable*. He uses it repeatedly, especially when faced with the fact that the hero of the story, Westley, is pursuing (and catching up with) the bad guys. Finally, another character, the swashbuckling Inigo Montoya, remarks to Vizzini, "That word. I do not think it means what you think it means."

It's a subtle joke about how slippery language is. Vizzini is not using the word improperly but maybe a bit carelessly: once or twice he says "inconceivable" when it might have been more accurate to say "impossible" or, better yet, "highly unlikely." But Montoya's line is funny because he might be thinking of how the word could mean something else entirely: rather than the sense of unimaginable, it can have a more physical meaning of infertile, which is the literal sense of being incapable of conceiving.

Language is a messy business. Think of the word *bark*. Is it something a dog does, a tree has, or a type of boat? It all depends on the context. Similarly, when we say we love chocolate, we love our country, we love our children, and we love our spouse, each usage of the word *love* is different, in a subtle but very real way.

Like it or not, the page is never blank. I love it when books are printed and a blank page has, at the bottom, one line of text: "This page intentionally left blank." Well, it's not blank, is it? It has a line announcing that it would have been blank, on purpose, but for that pesky line explaining the situation. That's kind of how the relationship between silence and language works in the human mind and heart.

When a child does not learn language skills, it can compromise his or her intelligence: the ability to function in our world. Like it or not, our souls are all pages printed with lots of text. Now comes the tricky part: trying to figure out what it all means.

And like *bark* and *love*, it often means different things; sometimes it's obvious, and sometimes it's subtle indeed.

> For my thoughts are not your thoughts,
>> nor are your ways my ways, says the LORD.
> For as the heavens are higher than the earth,
>> so are my ways higher than your ways
>> and my thoughts than your thoughts. (Isaiah 55:8–9)

Christianity has an unfortunate history of denigrating the human body. In the New Testament, for example, Saint Paul uses the Greek word for "flesh," σάρξ (*sarx*), to refer to the state of being sinful—a state that characterizes a person who does not know the saving love of Christ. Being lost in sin is a tragedy. But it's also a tragedy to equate *flesh* with *sin*. Sure, some sins are "fleshly" sins, like gluttony or sloth. But other sins, like pride or envy or hatred, arise from the mind as much as from the body. Those sins, it seems to me, are potentially even more dangerous than the fleshly sins.

For too long, Christians have suffered a subtle dualism—a way of seeing the world that regards the mind as better or holier than the body. This has led some Christians to becoming overly obsessed with bodily sin (especially regarding sexuality), which in turn has led other people to reject Christianity altogether, thinking it is just an outdated religion that is obsessed with sex. Meanwhile, I can't help but think that my stuck-in-the-headedness is at least partially a consequence of growing up in a culture that subtly denigrated the human body in favor of the mind.

Spirituality is, at least when it is truly healthy, holistic. The body, the soul, and the mind all are the beneficiaries of God's love and grace. Prayer and other spiritual disciplines are meant not only to heal us spiritually but mentally and physically as well. Learning to love our creatureliness—yes, even our fleshliness—is a consequence of choosing to orient our lives to the all-encompassing love of God.

Like Montoya, when I hear Christians talk trash about the flesh or the body or even sex, I think, "That word does not mean what you think it means." Saint Paul wants us to turn to love and away from sin. But love is more than just elevated thoughts or a pious value. Love gets expressed in embodied, down-to-earth ways. This includes loving the human body, loving the earth, loving the ordinary stuff of being human. It's not an anything-goes kind of love, of course. But we can say no to sin (including bodily sin as well as mental or spiritual sin) while still saying yes to the blessing that God has given us—the miracle that is the body.

Even when it gets sweaty-palm nervous at the thought of asking somebody cute out.

# Pagans and Druids
## and Buddhists—Oh My!

One of my favorite authors is the late Anglican priest Kenneth Leech, whose books were among the first ones I ever read on contemporary contemplative spirituality. I first heard of Ken back in the 1980s when someone recommended his book *Soul Friend* to me.[1] It's a survey of the history, meaning, and practice of spiritual companionship—how in one-on-one relationships we can nurture the depth and quality of our interior lives. Although Ken's writing can be a bit dry, his wisdom and spiritual insight spoke to me, and soon I was reading any book of his I could get my hands on, including titles like *True Prayer*, *We Preach Christ Crucified*, and *Experiencing God*. Over the years, Ken's writing played a significant role in my own discovery of, and appreciation for, the Christian contemplative tradition. It was one thing to marvel at the writings of past masters, even twentieth-century luminaries like Evelyn Underhill and Thomas Merton. But Kenneth Leech was a *living* contemplative master, which gave me hope that even I could enter the mysteries of a deeper life in Christ.

### "I Googled You. . . ."

Before he passed away, I had the privilege to meet Ken on several occasions, and we always had warm and insightful conversations on writing, faith, and various related topics. I particularly enjoyed his sense of humor. The first time we met, he recounted a story about giving a lecture at a seminary in America on the topic of race relations, a field in which he did extensive work for the Church of England. When the talk ended, one of the seminarians approached him to say how much he enjoyed the talk and then said something surprising.

"People must confuse you with the other Kenneth Leech," the student remarked.

A bit nonplussed, Ken asked who this "other Kenneth Leech" was.

The student replied, "You know, the one who has written all the books on spirituality."

Apparently, this poor seminarian couldn't equate a social-justice Christian with a contemplative-prayer Christian.

But yes, Leech the expert on racism and Leech the expert on mysticism were one and the same.

Ken recognized the humor in this story, but he also told me it made him a bit sad that people (or at least, this one priest-in-training) couldn't see the intimate connection between deep interior work and the importance of advocating for the reign of God—which naturally would include struggling against injustices like racism. Indeed, it was after this encounter that Ken wrote the book that I think is his masterpiece, *The Eye of the Storm*, which beautifully articulates the necessary connection between spirituality and social justice.

I would not presume to compare myself (as a writer, or as a person of faith) with someone of the stature and eminence of my hero Kenneth Leech. But it turns out that I, too, have had encounters with people that remind me of Ken's run-in with the seminarian. Nobody has ever suggested to me that they think there are two Carl McColmans running around, which I suppose is a very good thing; one of me is more than enough. But when someone takes a look at my list of books—especially the ones I wrote before I became a Catholic—the conversation sometimes veers into some unusual territory.

I was confirmed in the Catholic Church in 2005, and at that time I already was an established writer: I had published nine books and coauthored one other. These days most of those old books are out of print, but anyone with an internet connection can easily find used copies for sale (usually for about a penny plus shipping) on eBay or Amazon. A writer I once met named Isaac Bonewits lamented that a book you write long ago will forever be "following you about like an overly enthusiastic puppy for the rest of your life (and beyond)."[2] When he wrote those words, Isaac seemed to be saying that any authors who keep growing intellectually or spiritually will eventually be embarrassed by their past writing. I'm not particularly embarrassed by my earlier books, but they certainly do spark some unusual encounters with folks.

I know what's coming when I'm speaking at a retreat center somewhere and someone comes up to me and says, "When I heard you were going to lead our retreat, I googled you."

That usually leads to some variation of this question: "Are you the same Carl McColman who writes books about paganism?"

The conversation generally goes like this. First, I try to clarify matters. "Well, it's more accurate to say I *used to write* pagan books. The last one was written in 2004 and published in 2005. I haven't written books specifically for pagan readers since, well, I left the pagan world to become a Catholic."

"So you used to be a pagan."

"That's correct."

"You were into Wicca, Druidism, shamanism, goddess worship, all that stuff?"

"That's correct."

Now, at this point, our little interaction tends to go in one of two directions. Sometimes, the person will say "*Cool!*" and then confide in me how meaningful it has been for him or her to explore the spirituality of nature, of the divine feminine, and of indigenous rituals and practices. I am continually fascinated by how many people who identify as Christians—even won't-miss-a-Sunday church-going Christians—turn to alternative spiritual practices like Wicca and neo-paganism in order to nurture their need for a spirituality grounded in nature and in matter, a spirituality that is friendly to the body and sexuality and especially to a feminine face of God.

If you are not familiar with neo-paganism or Wicca, these are new religious movements that draw inspiration from the pre-Christian spiritualities of Europe and other parts of the world. These movements often emphasize the worship of a mother goddess in addition to (or instead of) a heavenly father. Or they may actually prefer to speak of divinity not in terms of a single god(dess) but many gods and goddesses. Persons who embrace pagan spiritualities typically exhibit deep reverence for the natural world and practice rituals and ceremonies that stress personal empowerment, a cyclical understanding of time and eternity, and a belief that human life is essentially good, deeply magical, and meant to be celebrated and enjoyed.

One does not need to be overly educated in Christian doctrine and theology to recognize how such a spirituality

is, in some ways, very much at odds with Christianity—
at least, with Christianity as it is often practiced by white
middle-class Americans, which often seems to be mostly
a watered-down Puritanism these days.

For me, exploring neo-paganism was an important if
unconventional chapter in my adult spiritual life. I first
encountered this kind of spirituality in college, cautiously
read about it for several years but then actively immersed
myself in its countercultural world long enough to write
several books about it. I eventually decided that whatever
it was that paganism was giving me I could find just as fully
by exploring the mystical tradition in Christianity. But like
Isaac Bonewits's perky pooch, the fact that I merrily wrote
books about paganism means it will always be a part of my
story. Which, on balance, may very well be a good thing.

I'll come back to the conversations I have with people
who think neo-paganism is cool later in this chapter. For
now, let's return to the conversation I'm having with the
person who googled me and discovered that I used to write
pagan books. Not everyone who makes this discovery necessarily finds it intriguing or amusing. There are those for
whom this discovery seems to be vaguely alarming, if not
downright frightening.

Here's the question I get asked: "But isn't all that stuff
evil?"

You see, *Wicca* is an old English word from which we
get the modern word *witch*. In other words, Wicca is a re-

ligious expression of witchcraft.[3] Once again, some people find this fascinating. Others find it creepy or even downright scary.

Now when someone asks me if pagan spiritualities are evil, I typically respond by saying, "I think it's dangerous to apply stereotypes to entire groups. Not all Christians are good, for example."

Most people get this, and they will readily acknowledge that money-grubbing TV preachers or clergy who abuse children are just two examples of Christians who undermine the integrity of our faith. The logic is simple. It's dangerous to say, "All Christians are good," when clearly that is not the case. But it also means it's just as inaccurate, not to mention unkind and unfair, to look at another spiritual path, even one like (gasp!) modern-day witchcraft, and therefore decide "All Wiccans are evil." It's a simplistic stereotype and even a young child can see the fallacy in that way of thinking.

### Respecting Other Faiths

I press the point further. "You could say the same thing about Muslims or Jews or Buddhists. Remember the Buddhist who shot those people at the DC Navy Yard? Human nature being what it is, you find good and evil in all walks of life, all groups of people. So, of course, there are some people who identify as pagans whose behavior I consider to be unethical if not sinful or evil. But many other pagans are good people who lead exemplary lives. As a direct outgrowth of their spirituality, they dedicate themselves to good things like building community or fostering environmental sustainability. Therefore I think we need to avoid using simplistic labels."

Sometimes, the person remains unconvinced, and will ask me, "Well, if it's not evil, why did you leave it? Why did you make the move from being a pagan to becoming a Catholic?"[4]

It's a reasonable question, especially for someone whose limited knowledge of paganism may have been distorted by religious prejudice. I try to answer it forthrightly, and clearly: "After exploring paganism for a number of years, I simply realized I didn't belong there. My heart belongs to Jesus Christ. For all the good I discovered in neopaganism, the fact that it isn't centered on Jesus and his radical teachings became an obstacle for me. Many pagans do regard Jesus as a venerable spiritual teacher, but nothing more than that: just one among many wisdom keepers. For me, it was a mistake to try to relativize Christ in that way. As the ancient Celtic Saint Columba once said, 'Christ is my Arch-Druid.' I needed a spiritual community and a rule of life that forms me directly in response to Christ's teaching and Christ's love. When I realized this, I had to act on my convictions, and so I returned to Christianity. Entering the Catholic Church made particular sense because of my interest in the contemplative, monastic, and mystical traditions within Christianity. But, really, Christ was the reason I came home."

I suppose if I were feeling a bit mischievous, I might also throw in that if I weren't a Christian, these days I'd probably be a Buddhist, for next to Christ, my sense is that the wisest spiritual teacher out there is probably Gautama Buddha. But I don't like to freak people out unnecessarily, so generally speaking I let that little remark slide. Nevertheless, sometimes the person who is interrogating me will say something like, "I saw online that you also do interfaith work."

"That's true. And out of that work, I remain deeply respectful of other faiths, *all* other faiths. Judaism and Buddhism, Hinduism and Islam, Wicca and Taoism, Sikhism and Shinto—as a contemplative, catholic Christian, it is my duty to be respectful of all religions, to respectfully disagree with what I think is wrong or misguided, but to just as respectfully affirm all that is good and true and beautiful. In every faith."

If the person I'm speaking with is a Catholic, or likely to respect Catholic teaching, I might add that the Catechism of the Catholic Church very explicitly affirms positive interfaith and interreligious dialogue. The Catechism suggests that part of the mission of every Christian should include "a respectful dialogue" with those who do not follow Christ. "Believers can profit from this dialogue by learning to appreciate better 'those elements of truth and grace which are found among peoples [of other faiths], and which are, as it were, a secret presence of God.' "[5]

Furthermore, a statement on "Dialogue and Proclamation" from the Pontifical Council for Inter-Religious Dialogue gives further detail on why Catholics (and, I would argue, other Christians) ought to reach out to those of other faiths. "While keeping their identity intact, Christians must be prepared to learn and to receive from and through others the positive values of their traditions. . . . Christians must remember that God has also manifested himself in some way to the followers of other religious traditions." This recognition takes humility: to give up on any kind of triumphalistic notion that only *my* religion has "all the answers." Seeking God through the wisdom of other faiths can be a profound way of deepening one's own spirituality. As the Pontifical Council puts it, "Far from weakening their own faith, true dialogue will deepen it."[6]

Back to my conversation with the person who googled me. "Let me get this straight. You wrote pagan books, but you are no longer a pagan. You realized paganism wasn't right for you, and that you love and follow Jesus Christ, but you don't run around calling paganism bad or evil because you believe it's important to respect other religions, even minority religions like paganism."

"That pretty much sums it up. Mind you, I don't believe 'anything goes.' I have a pretty solid grounding in the ethical norms of both Christianity and civil society, and so I quite naturally think some religious or spiritual practices are wrong. I think it's wrong to force women to wear burqas or to practice animal sacrifice like in Santeria or any other practice that is unjust, exploitative, or abusive. I think it's a mistake for someone to allow something like astrology to direct his or her life, or to place too much faith in an authoritarian spiritual leader, especially to the point of surrendering your will, your body, or your bank account. But to the extent that other religions or spiritual practices provide people with positive meaning, purpose, and ethical guidance, I believe as a Christian it's my job to be in dialogue with such faith, not in hostile opposition."

Sometimes a conversation like this will take a metaphysical turn. "Do you believe in the devil?"

"Evil is real. Just ask any slave or abused child or victim of trafficking or corruption. Whether 'the devil' is a sentient being or a mythical embodiment of evil is, to my mind, irrelevant. We must fight evil either way. But I also think we need to be careful to avoid stereotyping entire groups of people as 'good' or 'evil.' Instead we should simply oppose evil in whatever form it takes or whatever context it arises, and likewise we should support the good that can be found in almost any context or setting, no matter how surprising or unlikely."

Sometimes, if the person is being particularly honest with me, he or she will admit that it makes them uncomfortable that a Christian writer has such a strong interfaith dimension to their work. I think one of the interesting questions facing the Christian community in our time is this question of how Christians should relate to other faiths. Which reminds me of another story.

One time I was scheduled to give a Wednesday night talk at a large Episcopal Church in north Georgia, about an hour from where I live in the metro Atlanta area. During the drive, my phone rang—it was my brother from Florida. I had just spoken to him the day before to arrange to visit him and my sister-in-law later that year on a weekend when I was planning to attend a class at the St. Petersburg Shambhala Center. I was surprised to be getting a call from him so soon after our previous conversation.

"What's up?"

"Well, I'm worried about you."

"Why?"

"I'm worried that if word gets out that you take classes from Buddhists, it will sabotage your career as a Christian writer."

I laughed. My brother and sister-in-law are convinced agnostics, and it's hard to get them into a church even for a funeral. Needless to say, their perception of Christianity is shaped more by the secular media than by their own experience. "I don't think there's anything to worry about," I tried to reassure him. "Most of the people who read my books and attend my talks tend to be very open to interfaith dialogue, especially between Christianity and Buddhism."

I'm not sure I allayed all his misgivings, but we had to wrap up the call as I drove up to the church. I went inside, where dinner was being served prior to my talk. I grabbed a plate and sat down at a large round table with the pastor, the director of religious education (who had booked me to speak), and several other "pillars of the church." The conversation, which I joined mid-stream, had to do with the Dalai Lama's recent visit to Atlanta. It turned out that I was the only person at the table who had *not* gone to see him!

### Grounded Faith or Fear?

The moral of the story is that many Christians—yes, even pillars of the neighborhood church—are deeply interested in interfaith dialogue. Many devout and convinced Christians are nevertheless interested in hearing what figures like the Dalai Lama or Thich Nhat Hanh or Pema Chödrön have to say. That doesn't mean they're about to turn into Buddhists, even though some of them might go on to take a meditation class at a local Buddhist center. If they're like me (and I think most of them are), they feel pretty grounded in their fidelity to Jesus Christ. Doing interfaith work seems to go more smoothly when we do so out of a clear understanding of what we believe, what our values are, and what we understand about God and virtue and living a faithful life.

But, ironically, many other Christians find interfaith dialogue to be unsettling if not threatening. Sometimes this angst reaches the level of church leadership, as can be seen when in 1989 the Vatican's Congregation for the Doctrine of the Faith issued a statement called *Orationis Formas* or the "Letter to the Bishops of the Catholic Church on Some Aspects of Christian Meditation." It's basically a warning that Christians need to be careful when engaging in spiritual practices that are imported from other traditions, like zazen or transcendental meditation. This letter challenges Christians to be mindful about the real differences that exist between different religious traditions, but unfortunately, many people see a document like *Orationis* as simply a big stop sign: they interpret it to mean that when Christians practice Eastern meditation, they're doing something wrong or bad.

We need to find a way to make Christianity a tent big enough to include the folks who have no interest in non-Christian spirituality as well as those who are drawn to interfaith dialogue and interspiritual practice. Most important of all, we need to figure out a way to keep the interspiritualists and the non-interspiritualists from summarily rejecting or attacking one another. For this to happen, we need to find ways to help all Christians to become better grounded in their faith and in the rich spiritual traditions of the church. That's a tall order. But if we don't do it, we'll keep losing folks. It's mighty tempting to become "spiritual but not religious" when the religious people you know keep criticizing you for your innocent desire to learn and to understand.

Thankfully, not everyone has a visceral reaction against interfaith exploration—even when involving pagans and Wiccans and Druids. As I mentioned previously, I'm heartened at how some people find it fascinating that I used to be a pagan and that I wrote books on the topic. Some of those people may feel that way because, deep down inside, they want or need a spirituality that is more centered on earth than in heaven, on nature than on eternity, on affirming the body rather than trying to transcend it. I certainly can relate to these wants and needs. Of course, the contemplative dimension of Christianity includes teachings and stories that at least point to, if not explicitly affirm, a spirituality that is embodied, is erotic (in the best sense of the word), is playful, is filled with wonder, and that recognizes time is as sacred as eternity and the incarnate body is as holy as the abstract mind.

And I would wager that for every Christian who is drawn to neo-paganism (or Buddhism or some other faith tradition) because deep down they really want to convert away from Christianity, there are plenty of other people who feel drawn to these other faiths simply because they intuitively recognize that they are missing essential spiritual nutrients, and studying another tradition and learning its practices just might be the road to a greater spiritual maturity and health. In other words, they want to explore paganism or Buddhism or some other faith not in order to leave Christianity but actually to become a better Christian. Catholic theologian Paul Knitter even wrote a book called *Without Buddha I Could Not Be a Christian*. That title may be a bit overblown, but it points to the sentiment that I believe is motivating many Christians who today look for inspiration beyond just the Christian community.

It's all too easy to forget that there was a time in the Middle Ages when the writings of Thomas Aquinas were regarded as dangerous because he quoted Aristotle, the pagan Greek philosopher. Nowadays, conservative Christians love to quote Aquinas, which means we have largely accepted the fact that Christianity can be enhanced by wisdom from non-Christian or pre-Christian thinkers (like Aristotle or Plato). Now when someone in our time like Thomas Merton writes about the Buddha, isn't that more or less the same thing? And hopefully eight hundred years from now (if not much sooner) Christians will be just as comfortable drawing wisdom from the Buddha as we are today drawing wisdom from the Greek philosophers.

Can we as Christians truly and joyfully make room in our minds and hearts for the wisdom, the gifts, that can come to us from other spiritualities? And are we willing to do the work necessary to integrate those gifts into our own faith tradition, which means finding the ways in which the teachings of the Buddha resonate with the teachings of the desert fathers and mothers or the ways in which Wiccan ideas about the divine feminine resonate with the mystical teachings of Julian of Norwich, to offer just a few examples? *If* we are willing to do this work, then I believe we will reap great benefits, both individually and communally. On an individual level, our spirituality will grow rapidly and beautifully, and on a communal or even institutional level we might find that Christianity becomes just a little more appealing to some of the most intelligent and creative spiritual seekers among our children and grandchildren.

If Christians really took the time to excavate the treasures of our own heritage—in other words, the mystical and contemplative teachings that course through the centuries like a golden thread of divine love and light—the impulse to study Wicca or learn meditation from Buddhists will change dramatically. Not that it's a bad thing to explore these other paths, but when we recognize the treasures in our own history, then we are less needy in regard to other wisdom traditions.

Some people may read this and just start to object, "But pagans are functionally polytheists!" or "Buddhism is atheistic!" While statements like these are true on a level of simple fact, if they are used to derail positive interspiritual exploration, they represent an instance of spectacularly missing the point. Religion—any religion, even the "religionless religion" of the new age or the SBNR folks—consists of teachings, doctrines, propositions, and worldviews, but also of spiritual practices, mythological symbols, and exercises that help the followers of the religion to *live* and *embody* their spirituality. Christians, at least those who have learned to find joy and meaning in God's creativity, love, and mercy, are not going to opt for believing in multiple gods or in no god at all. When it comes to the ways in which adherents of different religions truly believe different things, we merely need to find a way to respect each other and be at peace with our differences.

## Holy Hospitality, Fervent Fidelity

At least in my experience, people are *not* drawn to different faiths because of ideas, doctrines, or propositions. Rather, they are drawn by images and symbols (like the goddess or the serene Buddha), by practices (like Zen or chanting), by a way of seeing the world (such as noticing the goodness of nature or discovering the silence beneath and within all sound). In other words, it may be our ideas and doctrines and dogmas that separate us, but it is our myths, our symbols, our spiritual exercises, and our ways of seeing (or hearing) that can help us find points of connection, of union, and of harmony. *That's what drives most interfaith explorers.* Christianity needs to step up to the plate and find ways to balance being faithful to our sacred story (the gospel, the radical teachings of Jesus) while also offering hospitality to the rich treasures of myth, symbol, image, vision, and practice that can be discovered in other faith contexts and that can enhance, rather than undermine, the beauty and power of Jesus's wisdom and ethical precepts.

This is a messy proposition. Hospitality is always a bit chaotic, whether it's inviting your crazy aunt home for Thanksgiving or figuring out a way to accommodate your Wiccan daughter-in-law at your grandson's First Communion. But from Jesus to the desert mothers and fathers to the Celtic saints and Saint Benedict, all the way down to Dorothy Day and Mother Teresa in recent years, *hospitality* has been a key element of Christian spirituality. It's high time we invite the Wiccans and Muslims and Buddhists over for tea. And see what happens.

And for the person who worries that all this interfaith hobnobbing is just a little too messy, a little too boundary-less: believe it or not, but I want to affirm you, too. I want to affirm anyone who really wants to be radically faithful to Christ. I think we need, as a community, to find ways to affirm both the hospitality of interspirituality and the fidelity of remaining exclusively anchored in Christian teaching and practice. Fidelity and hospitality need each other, just like Mary and Martha need each other or science and art need each other. Some of us are better at faithfulness and others are better at hospitality. To keep the body of Christ healthy, let's find ways to affirm both of these styles of discipleship even if that means living in an ongoing creative tension.

## Let Him Kiss Me
## with the Kisses of His Mouth

It took a friendship with a Muslim to teach me how to pray like a Christian.

As I wrote the previous sentence, I smiled because of how I met my Muslim friend who taught me so much about prayer. His name is Kemal; he's a Sufi and a Turkish immigrant who lives here in Atlanta. We were introduced through our mutual friend, Ben Campbell Johnson, who was a larger-than-life figure in the Atlanta interfaith community especially during the years following the tragedy of 9/11.

I had met Ben through a mutual friend, and he interviewed me for a public-access cable TV show he hosted called *The Experience of God*. This interview took place a few years after I became a Catholic, and of course I wanted to talk about Catholicism, but Ben kept steering the conversation back to my time exploring neo-paganism. I soon realized that for Ben, interfaith dimensions of spirituality mattered at least as much as plumbing the depths of one's "home" faith.

Ben was a huge teddy bear of a man, a gentle octogenarian with an ever-present smile and a twinkle in his eyes. He spoke with a beautiful Southern drawl; I don't think I ever heard him sing, but I suspect he had a gorgeous baritone. He clearly loved God, and because he loved God so much, he loved all of God's children, without bothering to fuss over what religious tribe any particular person was connected to. God loves everyone, and that was good enough for Ben.

## Names Before Labels

A few months after *The Big Book of Christian Mysticism* was published, I was invited to speak at an interfaith conference in Portland, Oregon. I was still pretty new to the so-called speaking circuit and had never been exposed to gatherings that were explicitly interfaith in nature. The event organizer wanted me to talk about Celtic spirituality and its relationship to my exploration of both paganism and Christianity. So off I flew to the West Coast and had a wonderful weekend rubbing elbows not only with pagans and Christians, but Muslims, Jews, and adherents of Eastern spiritual paths. Everyone's hospitality and warmth touched me deeply, and I returned to Atlanta convinced that I wanted to get connected to the interfaith community in my hometown.

Ben was the obvious link to that world, so I sent an email and enthusiastically asked, "Can you introduce me to some Muslims?"

He very kindly replied that he would be happy to introduce me to, at first, one person, his friend Kemal. And while he didn't say as much, I got the hidden message: *Let's talk about "friends" and address people by their name, not their religious or ethnic label.*

Shortly thereafter I met Kemal when Ben asked me to participate in a small interfaith spirituality weekend taking place at a local Disciples of Christ Church. Over the course of the weekend five speakers would present spiritual insights from each of their faiths: a rabbi would lead off on Friday evening, followed by Kemal (representing Islam) on Saturday morning, a Zen priest that afternoon, and a Hindu teacher that evening; I would round out the weekend by sharing some thoughts on Christian spirituality Sunday morning. I didn't have to think twice about this opportunity.

A few days later, the five speakers gathered for a meeting with Ben and representatives from the hosting church. We talked about our dreams for making this weekend event truly meaningful and helpful for anyone who attended. We talked about our shared interest in interfaith dialogue and interspirituality. Everyone was articulate, thoughtful, and clearly committed both to the treasures of their own faith tradition and also to the hope of helping to create a world where we could all live in harmony.

About an hour into the meeting, Kemal excused himself and stepped outside the room. The conversation continued, and Ben made a comment to the effect that Kemal would rejoin us as soon as he was done praying.

I thought about all the times I had ignored or blown off the rhythm of Christian daily prayer because I was "too busy" or had some sort of work-related commitment.

A few days later Kemal and I made plans for me to join him and his imam for dinner at the local Turkish Center. I drove to the north suburbs of Atlanta where a feast of hummus, baba ghanoush, tabouli, and falafel awaited me. (When I had shyly informed Kemal that I was a vegetarian, he promptly replied, "No problem!") After that hearty meal, we talked about how participating in the interfaith community deepened our commitment to our respective faiths. Finally, I blurted out, "I was so impressed the other day when you stepped out of the meeting to pray."

He smiled. "A Muslim commits to praying five times a day." He explained the rhythm of daily prayer, which seemed to clearly parallel Christian monastic prayer—a daily cycle of prayer known as the Divine Office or the Liturgy of the Hours. This daily program of fixed-hour prayer incorporates psalms, canticles, Scripture readings, intercessions, and other prayers to enable a person or a community to literally pray throughout the day. Most people associate the Divine Office with the daily chanting of monks and nuns, but in fact it is meant for all Christians, lay and ordained, monastic and secular. Different forms of the Divine Office exist, usually connected to the various churches within Christianity: there are Orthodox versions of the Office, Catholic versions, as well as Presbyterian and Anglican and Lutheran Liturgies. Other variations of the Divine Office are associated with particular monastic or religious communities, so you can find a Benedictine Liturgy, a Celtic Liturgy, and so forth.

The Catholic Liturgy of the Hours consists of five to seven "offices" of prayer for each day (the prayers for midday can be prayed all at once or broken into three smaller offices for midmorning, noon, and midafternoon). Clearly, very similar in structure, if not in content, to the daily prayers of Muslims.

As a Lay Cistercian, my rule for praying the Liturgy of the Hours is almost embarrassingly minimal: my community asks me to pray at least once a day. I'm not proud to admit it, but even this low bar was frequently too high for me.

And here my Muslim friend was putting me to shame, faithfully praying five times a day, day in and day out—even if it meant excusing himself from an important meeting.

I confided in him how difficult it was for me to pray even once a day. He smiled, and his response was filled with grace. "Muslims have learned that we really must develop a habit of praying throughout the day when we are children," he said. "If you're much more than ten years old when you start, chances are you will struggle with it your entire life."

Hmm. I had never even heard of the Liturgy of the Hours until I was in my early thirties and didn't make a commitment to daily prayer until I was in my late forties. What hope was there for me?

"God is gracious," was Kemal's simple and elegant comment. In other words, my hope for cultivating a meaningful daily prayer practice begins and ends entirely in and with God. It is by God's graciousness that a self-conscious, overly analytical guy like me has any prayer life at all. And the key to making prayer a regular part of my life? Simply put, it's all about my willingness to trust God to lead the way.

Kemal took out his phone and playfully remarked, "The smartphone is a Muslim's best friend." He showed me several apps that help him to know what time to pray, along with helping him to figure out the direction to Mecca (since Muslims worldwide pray facing that way).

I had downloaded some Christian apps geared toward the Divine Office and showed them to Kemal as well. With an increasing sense of humility, I realized that I had everything I needed to pray every day: access to the common prayers of my faith community, the gift of good health and a job that gives me the flexibility to pray, and—despite my lack of discipline—a heart that desires intimacy with God.

## Rote Prayers Are Not the Problem

Oh, how I wish I could write that suddenly my prayer life took off and now I pray with the daily discipline of a Trappist. But the truth is much humbler and messier. Some days are better than others. I still only manage to pray the complete Liturgy when I am on retreat, supported by the established routine of the monks or nuns wherever I happen to be staying. The rest of the time: well, on my good days I get in morning prayer and maybe compline. And on my far-too-frequent not-as-good days, well, let's just say I cast myself on the mercy of God.

Isn't that, after all, the scandal of grace: that God loves me even when I don't manage (or bother) to pray for a day or even for days at a time? Now, in my own defense, I pray in some shape or form most days: whether it's begging for a parking spot when I'm late to an appointment or taking a few minutes to reflect on a meaningful passage I've found in Scripture or a mystical classic, or even haranguing God with whatever problem or anxiety I happen to be obsessing over at the time. And I'm much more disciplined with the prayer of contemplative silence—a daily practice of simply resting in a heartful place where only my breath or a repeated prayer word stimulates my mind. And I know that for many people, prayer is not so much something we *say* as it is *a way we live*. "Make my life a prayer to you," sang the old Christian rock band called 2nd Chapter of Acts. Is reading rote prayers out of a book really that important when what most of us want is that sense of *living in God's presence*?

It's so tempting to say no. It's not the ritual that matters: it's the condition of our hearts. In fact, given how easy it is to just go through the motions when praying rote prayers, it seems like they just get in the way.

On the surface, that seems to be pretty logical. But when I think about it, I keep wondering: Why, then, are rote prayers and rituals found in basically every major spiritual tradition?

Just up the street from where I live is the Atlanta Shambhala Center, where Buddhists and other meditators gather every morning for an hour of sitting and walking meditation. Every day they began their practice with three chants, the same three chants, day in and day out.

Meanwhile, Christian monks all over the world pray a similar cycle of psalms and canticles, day in and day out. And while it might take two weeks or so to get through all 150 psalms, some of the canticles—like the Benedictus and the Magnificat, both from the Gospel of Luke—get prayed every single day.

And Muslim daily prayer is rote. As is the Shema prayed by observant Jews.

This kind of structured daily prayer has been going on for centuries. If rote prayer is really so inimical to a meaningful and intimate relationship with God, wouldn't somebody have figured that out long before our generation? Why is it only in our time—a time shaped by relentless mass media, the droning noise of broadcast television and the internet, the endless blare of amplified music and social media—that we have suddenly decided that formal prayers are a waste of time?

Which leads me to a simple but compelling thought: maybe it's not the rote prayer that gets in the way of intimacy, but it's the ego constantly telling us that rote prayers are useless. *That's* what gets in the way.

And maybe, just perhaps, the reason why the human ego finds rote prayer so boring is because the more a person prays, the smaller the ego becomes. And the ego won't go down without a fight.

### Learning the Habit of Love

The Christian philosopher James K. A. Smith wrote a book called *You Are What You Love: The Spiritual Power of Habit* in which he makes the case that human beings are shaped as much by what we love as by what we believe. Descartes proclaimed, "I think, therefore I am," but Smith would respond that it is in our *loving* that we truly are human. However, what's tricky is that what we *think* we love and what we *actually* love might not always be the same thing. We can be pretty good at tricking ourselves. Smith points out that we are also creatures of habit, and our habits, more than our thoughts, reveal what truly matters to us—in other words, what we love.

We might *say* that faith in God is what really matters to us, but our actions betray that we really place much more trust in our career and our financial portfolio than we do in God. We might say that our spouse and children are the most important relationships in our lives, but we spend far more time on social media chatting with our college drinking buddies than we devote to the people we live with. It's not always comfortable to admit it, but what we think we love and what we actually love are not always the same. The old proverb had it right: actions speak louder than words. And we tend to encode our actions in our habits.

Let's explore this further: we say we worship God, but at times we worship anything but God. To see this, we need to start by acknowledging that we are capable of worshiping almost anything.

One time when I was at a gathering of neo-pagans, I made a comment about how pagans worship the goddess. A Wiccan high priestess who was hosting the meeting bristled at my words. "We don't *worship* anything," was her icy comment. I suppose she was reacting to a religious worldview that equates worship with submission or obeisance. But I intuitively disagreed with her then, and I still do—because to worship someone or something, at heart, is simply to love and honor the object of our worship. In the seventeenth century, wedding vows included this delicious line: "With this Ring I thee wed, with my Body I thee worship, and with all my worldly Goods I thee endow: In the Name of the Father, and of the Son, and of the Holy Ghost. Amen."

We're not particularly accustomed to the idea that a husband worships his wife with his body, which sounds vaguely blasphemous to our post-Puritan ears. But it's a reminder that the line between love and worship is quite thin indeed, and we did not always reserve the concept of worship just for divine beings. (We also used to address some public officials as "Your Worship," presumably meaning "Your Worthiness.")

So, anyone who is even vaguely religious in our day will protest that they only worship God. But their habits might reveal that they are much more accustomed to worshiping money or material goods or entertainment or sports or a certain social or political philosophy, or perhaps even nothing more than themselves.

Now: back to my friend Kemal and daily prayer and the Christian Liturgy of the Hours. I think the reason why the ego (or let me keep this personal: this is certainly true of *my* ego, and you can decide for yourself if this applies to yours as well) gets bored in a hurry when presented with routine, rote, repeated prayers is simply because *when we pray habitually, we are recalibrating our heart to love and worship God instead of the ego*. Daily prayer, in other words, is an embodied practice of slowly transforming narcissism into God worship. It's embodied; it's not just something we think about but something we do, day in and day out. It's slow: we can *think* about transforming from narcissism to God worship and decide to do it, but unless we show up, day after day, for the unglamorous work of daily prayer, then our thoughts are basically meaningless because the ego is still running the show. It takes time: perhaps even an entire lifetime, but certainly many years, for the slow work of transforming self-love to God-love to take place. And I suspect that on this side of eternity, the job is never fully done, not even for saints, not even for someone who's been praying faithfully for half a century or more.

Should we give up in despair, then? That's the old ego talking again. "If it's going to take a lifetime to truly learn how to love God, why bother? Why not simply enjoy life today?" It's just another dodge. It ignores Jesus's simple promise: "seek first the kingdom of heaven and God's righteousness, and all the other things you need will be given to you as well" (see Matthew 6:28–33). In other words, we're not asked to be miserable while we recalibrate our hearts (that is to say, while we pray our way into loving God). Quite the contrary. Christianity is a faith that dares to acknowledge that creation, and being creative, is good and therefore to be enjoyed within the reasonable boundaries of what is truly loving, not just for God but for other people as well. So yes, indeed, simply enjoy life today *and* anchor that enjoyment in the context of regular daily prayer, the kind of prayer that slowly transforms a self-centered heart into a God-centered one.

### Like Kissing

All this leads to another question. *How* do we pray?

Especially for those of us (nearly all of us) Christians who were not exposed to a practice of daily prayer as children, how do we pick it up now? How do we learn to pray every day, to engage in the slow work of transforming self-love into God-love, of building a new habit that worships God, and out of that love finds healthy and appropriate ways to love others as we love ourselves?

When I worked for the monks at their abbey store, people would come in to buy the Liturgy of the Hours. Now the complete Catholic Liturgy of the Hours comes in a beautiful four-volume set, available with either vinyl or leather binding, in either regular or large print type. The least expensive edition costs about $150, and the large-print leather set will set you back $200. For most folks, the Liturgy is not exactly an impulse buy. Presumably, if you're going to buy a copy of the Liturgy, you want to actually use it.

In other words, prayer matters to you.

But I discovered something over the years I worked at the store. As Kemal said, we really need to learn daily prayer when we're still a child. But most of us, as children, mostly just learned how to watch TV and be good consumers. (I don't mean to disparage our parents; most of them were doing the best they could in a society that has long forgotten what it means to pray every day.) Many Christians, even devout ones, have no idea what it means to pray every day—how to do it, how to deal with distractions, how to manage feelings of boredom or restlessness, how to be present with words we don't understand or ideas about God that we disagree with. And then there is the practical question of navigating these big fat prayer books: learning how to locate specific prayers in various parts of an eight hundred-page book, marking them with different colored ribbons, and then praying them in the correct sequence, day after day.

Sure, we know how to "talk to God" all the time on subjects ranging from complaining about our boss to fervent requests for peace or a better relationship with the kids. But when it comes to the daily Liturgy, most people feel utterly at a loss. The Liturgy seems to be a hot, complicated mess, and many folks find it intimidating.

They would never admit this to their priest, their confessor, or their spiritual director. But the nerdy middle-age guy running a cash register at the monastery bookstore? They'll confide in *him*.

So people would admit to me that they *want* the blessing of daily prayer in their lives, and they recognize that the Liturgy is an ancient tried-and-true system for weaving regular prayer into the hours of each day. But when they would pick up the fat volumes of the Liturgy or even visit a website that explains "How to pray the Divine Office," they would end up confused and befuddled.

Patiently, I would try to explain that it's just a steep learning curve, but once you get the hang of it, the Liturgy is a delight (which I know is true, even though I'm such a slacker myself when it comes to disciplined prayer). I'd invoke G. K. Chesterton, who said, "if a thing is worth doing, it is worth doing badly." In other words, you don't have to be a "pro" to pray the Liturgy (which is to say, you don't have to be a priest or a monk or a nun). And it's certainly okay to be less than perfect when you do it.

I'd say something like this:

If you make a mistake or two, turning to the wrong page or praying Wednesday's prayers on a Thursday, so what? We learn from our mistakes. If no child would ever touch a guitar unless he or she could immediately sound like Eric Clapton, well, it would soon be the end of music. It takes hours or months of making noise before the music begins to flow and years of dedicated practice to truly become a virtuoso. Even Eric Clapton himself practiced for hours a day, for years, before he became the guitar hero he now is.

Therefore, to become proficient at prayer, we have to begin by being sloppy and not very good at it. And then we have to persevere.

In other words, if you want to pray every day, then pick up the Divine Office book and another little guidebook that tells you which pages to turn to on any given day; turn to those pages, and *pray*. That's what matters.

Often, the person thinking about buying this expensive Liturgy book would look at me, almost suspiciously, as if it really couldn't be *that* easy.

So I would try again. And the first time I hit on this idea, I saw the person's eyes light up with understanding. Here's what I would say:

"Prayer is like kissing. When you were thirteen years old, or however old you were, and you had a crush on somebody in your class and the two of you would take walks together and then hold hands and then finally you found the courage to kiss. Neither one of you knew how to kiss, now, did you? But somehow you muddled through."

For you see, prayer *is* like kissing.

Everyone kisses a little differently. Some people are prim and proper with their kisses, others sultry and sexy. Some kisses are quiet and introspective, others are vibrant and passionate. And yes, there is even such a thing as an angry kiss or a sad kiss or an I'm-in-the-middle-of-a-meltdown kiss.

But every kiss is communication. And nobody ever gave us a book with a title like *Kissing for Dummies*. I don't think such a book could be written anyways.[1] I know teenagers can get nervous about kissing—teenagers can get nervous about everything—but the best antidote to feeling nervous about kissing is, well, to go ahead and kiss the person you want to kiss (and who wants to kiss you).

When we were kids facing our first kiss, we got nervous over things like "What if I have bad breath?" "What if he or she has bad breath?" "What if it turns out to be gross or creepy?" "What do I do with my nose?" and so forth. But that's where this analogy breaks down because when it comes to talking about how prayer is like kissing, we're talking about God here. Prayer is a kiss *from God*. When we pray, even if we're just reciting printed words in a book, we are showing up to accept the kiss of God's love. And if it makes us nervous, well, the best way to get over that is to just do it.

Come to think of it, if it makes us bored or angry or distracted or whatever, once again the best antidote to all those unprayerful feelings is to just get on with the praying.

Prayer is like kissing. We kiss because we love—or at the very least because we like—the person we're kissing. A kiss is always a sign of desire, whether it's sexual desire, loving desire, or even just the desire to foster or maintain a close friendship. On a human level this is messy and imperfect: nobody wants a kiss from somebody they don't like. But on the level of spirituality, we are already promised that God simply *loves* us. I would even go so far as to say that God *adores* us. In traditional religious language, *adoration* is something reserved for God alone: "I adore God; I cherish my wife." It makes a kind of poetic sense to consider that one of the reasons we ought to adore God alone is simply because of how beautifully God adores us. The word *adoration* literally means "to speak to," so when we adore God and God adores us, we speak words of love to one another. And that is the heart of prayer.

So why pray every day—especially if it's prayer out of a book? You're not telling God anything God doesn't already know (well, frankly, that's true even when you're praying spontaneously the words out of your own heart). But when you offer those words to God, *God speaks to you through them*. It's two-way communication. The Liturgy of the Hours *forms* us, helping us to slowly claim and reclaim the fact that we were created in God's image and likeness: a fundamental theological fact that most of us have thoroughly forgotten.

Make no mistake: I'm all for the spontaneous prayers that well up from the hidden places in our hearts. I believe God speaks to us through those prayers as well as through any traditional prayers printed in a book. When we bring to God our thanksgiving, our vulnerability, our need, our anger, our sorrow and contrition, and our desire to see others blessed and healed, God is not surprised, but God uses those prayers to form *us*, slowly and gradually, into people who are grateful, courageous, repentant, compassionate, and worshipful. It's a beautiful thing to slowly and gradually be transformed into a person of prayer. But you can't learn it from a book or master it after a weekend workshop. It requires showing up, day in and day out, over a lifetime.

Okay, one last thought, for all of us who never learned how to pray every day as a child. We have a big handicap as we run the race of faith. We are late getting started, and we will likely be spotty and messy with our prayer for the rest of our lives. It is so tempting to give in to despair and resign ourselves to the fact that we will never amount to much spiritually. Once again, that's the ego talking. Remember, God is the God of heaven as well as earth. What we begin here on earth does not get finished until we enter the silence of eternity. You and I will likely spend the rest of our earthly prayer lives as the most humble of beginners. But we are kissing the one who loves us perfectly. Because it is *God* to whom we pray, our prayer is perfect no matter how late we get started or how distracted we are or how many days we miss. We're going to miss days, maybe even weeks and months, out of our daily prayer practice. What do we do then? It's simple: always begin again.

# It's the End of the World
# as We Know It (and I Feel Fine)

When I was a small boy, adults always asked me what I wanted to be when I grew up

I found this question fraught with peril.

In the 1960s, gender stereotypes still defined how children's books and TV shows talked about grown-up work. All the jobs offered to boys struck me as way too dangerous. I could be a policeman or a firefighter or a soldier or a pilot or a doctor.

Even when I was four years old, I thought each of these was a terrible choice.

Why would I want to be a doctor if it meant exposing myself to sick people all the time? No doubt I would quickly catch some sort of rare tropical malady and die a lingering death, complete with purple blotches on my nose.

My dad was a pilot, but I didn't see much point in following in his footsteps since planes could crash and I would probably meet my end in a fiery blaze of horror.

Speaking of fire, no way would I willingly walk into a house with roaring flames and poisonous smoke surrounding me on all sides.

Policeman? Yeah, right. Criminals shooting at me all day long? It made no sense to me. As for being a soldier, that sounded even worse since it meant sooner or later an entire army of enemies would be taking aim at me.

From the vantage point of midlife, I can look back on my childish fears and smile. I chuckle at how silly my immature thinking must look to my readers; it certainly seems rather foolish to me. But when I was just a little boy, the anxiety I felt was only all too real.

Every time I would meet a new adult—usually some friend of my parents—I got asked that same terrible question. I had no choice but to come up with *something*.

I gave the matter a lot of thought, and finally I hit on what seemed to me the most foolproof (and fail-safe) career choice.

"When I grow up, I want to be a painter," I announced to my family one day.

"A painter?" my mother asked, her brow furrowed. "Do you mean an artist?"

"No, not an artist," I tried to explain. "A *painter*. Like someone who paints houses."

I don't think my parents quite knew what to make of my surprisingly modest ambition. Finally my dad said, "Son, why do you want to be a painter?"

"Well," I replied, "It's *safe*."

"Safe?"

I went on to share my childish logic to show how I decided all the other potential jobs were far too hazardous to consider.

Finally my brother John interrupted me.

"But painting's not safe either! What if you fall off the ladder? What if you mistake a can of paint for your drink, and you accidentally drink the paint and poison yourself?"

I was aghast.

Even the seemingly benevolent vocation of house painting, it turned out, was strewn with hidden dangers.

### Conflict and Confidence

I wish I could say that my brief flirtation with the home-improvement industry was the last time I made choices just to avoid facing what scares me, but alas, that was the first of many anxiety-driven moves I've made. Fear has been a loyal, if unwelcome, companion for most of my life.

During my school years, I lacked social confidence; I was the shy kid that usually played by myself and preferred books to sports. I've already shared how adolescence immersed me in a new realm of terror: when I noticed that I "liked" girls and saw my friends start to pair off into boyfriends-and-girlfriends, my fearfulness kicked into overdrive.

If it wasn't for the cute girl I mentioned previously, who worked part-time as a cashier at the local book'n'card shop where I shopped all the time—who apparently had a thing for the quiet, nervous type, for she kept flirting with me until I discovered that I could talk to her without my head exploding—I might have ended up fulfilling my childhood fantasy of becoming a hermit in the woods.

Even more troubling, I made educational and vocational choices because I was far more afraid of the negative consequences of what might go wrong than I was confident of the likelihood of success (and thereby willing to take the risk). I think I was well into adulthood before I even grasped the concept of a prudent or reasonable risk.

There's a theory that a particular part of the brain, the amygdala, controls and manages our fear response. Apparently it is just a theory, and controversial at that, but I'm not a neuroscientist, so for the sake of this chapter we'll just go with it. I seem to have been "blessed" at birth with an overactive and maybe supersized amygdala.

Where other people see "risk," I see "certain disaster." Where other people see "basically safe but lots of fun," I see "fraught with menace and not worth taking the chance."

It really is a *way of seeing.* Over the years, I've slowly come to recognize that my fear thermostat seems to have been set way too high at birth. My mom once told me that my birth was difficult, so maybe from the get-go I learned that life is dangerous and I needed to play it safe. I don't know if that is a psychological problem, a spiritual problem, or even some sort of weird brain chemistry imbalance. At this point in my life, it really doesn't matter. But in my childhood years, not only was I profoundly fearful, but I never managed to communicate to my parents or teachers just how frightened I felt by so much of life. And even if I had, I'm not sure that my blue-collar family would have offered me any remedy other than to buck up and be a little man.

In case you're wondering, yes, I eventually did work with a therapist, actually four therapists over about a twenty-five-year period, and slowly acquired a number of life skills that, while not eradicating or eliminating my fear, at least helped me to manage it and to make choices based more on my desires than on simply trying to avoid my imaginary tragedies.

I read plenty of pop-psychology books over the years that gave me insight into my confidence-deficit personality and provided me with new ways to approach life in more hopeful or creative ways. One of my favorites was Susan Jeffers's *Feel the Fear and Do It Anyway*. Even the title gave me a new perspective. Jeffers suggests that anxiety is a normal feeling whenever we try something new. Since trying new things is essential for a life well lived, therefore a certain amount of fearful feelings actually is a good thing.

Maybe you figured that out when you were five years old, but for me it was a revelation at age thirty.

After all that therapy and reading, have I simply embraced life with gusto, consigning fearfulness to the dustbin of my past? Not entirely. Old habits die hard, and overactive amygdalae don't go down without a fight.

Since this is the last chapter of the book, I thought I would end it with an unteachable lesson that I am still in the process of learning.

This lesson involves writing (which, eventually, replaced house painting as my career of choice) and conflict (which, frankly, I would like as little to do with as possible).

Whenever I teach a writing class, whether my students aspire to write fiction or nonfiction, we always talk about how important conflict is to telling a story.

If you don't have conflict, you don't really have much of a story.

Where would Sherlock Holmes be without Professor Moriarty? Or Harry Potter without Voldemort? Or Aslan without the White Witch? Great stories require not only great heroes and heroines, but also great villains.

But as someone who sees the world through fear-colored glasses, I learned pretty young to avoid conflict at all costs. Even as a writer. I discovered long ago I wasn't interested in writing about most forms of human conflict. One writing mentor when I was in graduate school told me, "publishers only want books about rich people being mean to each other." I think that was the point when I decided not to pursue fiction writing as a vocational choice.

I wasn't interested in writing about war or violence or abuse or even politics.

But whether I like it or not, writers need to write about conflict in some shape or form.

Many folks think Winston Churchill was a great man, but Neville Chamberlain is more or less forgotten. (Chamberlain, Churchill's predecessor, was the British prime minister whose policy was to avoid fighting Germany in the years leading up to World War II.) Nowadays, historians are more kind to Chamberlain because they recognize that Britain simply wasn't ready to go to war with Germany in the 1930s. But especially right after the war, Chamberlain was reviled as an "appeaser," unlike the more courageous Churchill, who led the fight to defeat the Nazis.

But there is another side to refusing a fight than appeasement or avoidance. Think of Mahatma Gandhi or Martin Luther King Jr. They were nonviolent activists. In other words, instead of *evading* conflict, they actively sought ways to *resolve* conflict without resorting to violence, hostility, or force.

I want to approach conflict in my writing more like Gandhi than like Chamberlain. In other words, I am mostly interested in the question of how we resolve conflict. When I began to write spiritual nonfiction, I realized I was primarily interested in the most foundational conflict of all—the conflict that each person experiences in his or her own heart.

We all hunger for God, and yet we all resist God. We all want to be holy or good people, and yet we all have a selfish or narcissistic streak. We all seek silence and prayer, and yet most of us do plenty to avoid the conditions for living a prayerful life.

In other words, the conflict that interested me the most as a writer is the conflict that each person has deep within—between wanting God and *not* wanting God.

That, it seemed to me, is more important than just about any other kind of conflict I could write about. Because, I reasoned, if we work on resolving our *inner* conflicts, then it will be easier to face whatever *outer* conflicts come our way.

But not every editor I have worked with has seen things this way.

I've had editors, both online and in traditional publishing, suggest to me that if I really wanted to make a difference with my writing, then I needed to address the challenges (and conflicts) that most people face in their ordinary, day-to-day life.

This meant writing about family dynamics. Or about workplace issues. Or about—*perish the thought*—current events. And politics.

Every time I would receive a request like this from an editor, I'd turn into a four-year-old boy wanting to paint houses.

## There Are Conflicts We Cannot Avoid

"In polite company, you never discuss religion or politics."

This was something my parents drilled into me when I was a child. However, at least in the privacy of our own home, we were not very "polite," as least as far as politics was concerned. On occasion my dad and one of my brothers would get into a discussion, and the discussion would become a debate, and the debate would become an argument, and the argument would devolve into a shouting match.

As the youngest child, I pretty much stayed out of it. But I learned my dislike for conflict around the family dinner table. I figured if *this* is what talking politics led to, well, I'd just as soon stay polite and keep my mouth shut, thank you very much.

As an adult, I now see things a bit differently. I realized "nice people don't discuss politics" is actually a marker of social privilege. It only makes sense when you have it good enough that it doesn't matter whether you keep your views to yourself or not. Sometimes, we need to have uncomfortable conversations; otherwise, nothing will ever change.

But keep in mind, I'm someone who finds it easier to be afraid than to trust. To willingly take on a fight—even a verbal debate—requires at least some confidence; if nothing else, the belief that your views are worth sharing with others.

Every time someone would ask me to make my work more relevant to the "real issues" of the day, I'd make up an excuse, usually along these lines: I was writing timeless books about eternal topics like mysticism or contemplation. The last thing I wanted to do was to start bringing in political or social views that would just turn off half of my potential readers. After all, silent prayer is just as important for conservatives as for liberals, for Democrats as for Republicans. In fact, I believed that if someone's political values were messed up, they *needed* contemplative prayer to help them recalibrate their hearts and their minds to a healthier or saner perspective.

In other words, the last thing I wanted to do was to limit my audience by catering to just one particular viewpoint.

But the requests kept coming.

Often when I would meet a contemplative author or teacher who I respected, I would ask for advice for my work as a writer. More than once, my elder would say to me, "People are concerned about how to be a contemplative in today's political climate. We need writers who are willing to address this question."

Certainly over the last twenty years—with the 9/11 attacks, the rise of the internet and social media, the increasingly contentious nature of much political journalism, and then the growing sense of division between so-called liberals and conservatives—it seems that American political life seemed to be getting more toxic than ever.

Sigh. Even contemplatives sometimes get called into the fray.

I was talking to a monk the other day who is a lovely man and, I believe, a true mystic and a truly holy person. And, like most of us, he has strong political views. While we were talking, I joking called myself a "radical moderate."

"What do you mean?" he asked, his voice tinged with suspicion.

"I mean that I recognize that for the good of our country we need to restore a way of being political that doesn't involve so much hatred, so much name-calling, so much attacking not just ideas but the people who hold the ideas. We need to find a way to love the people on the other side."

"But only one side is telling the truth!" he objected.

Therein lies the problem.

I'm not going to tell you how this man votes, but I can assure you that there are plenty of people on both sides of our political divide who feel exactly the same way he does. "My side is telling the truth, and their side is filled with propaganda." Or lies, or "fake news"—whatever you want to call it.

Unless and until we can reach a place where each side can admit that maybe, just *maybe*, the other side *might* have a point worth considering now and then, we will remain prisoners of our own divisions.

I'm not suggesting that anyone should abandon his or her political views. Despite my joke, I actually do have fairly strong political views, and I doubt if anyone who knew my views would call me a centrist. But I *am* a centrist when it comes to the crying spiritual need of our time, which is to restore the promise of democracy—where we all work together to find creative ways to manage our conflicts rather than deciding that the only acceptable solution is the complete dominance of "my" party or beliefs over "theirs."

And given how intense some of our conflicts are, I am convinced the only way our society can learn to manage our conflicts is through a deeply contemplative approach. Where we value listening over shouting and asking questions over demanding compliance. Where we begin by remembering that all people have dignity and that even the most humble persons among us might have something valuable to say. Where we recognize that deep-seated conflicts are not going to be solved overnight and, at the same time, real people who are suffering require real relief now, not at some imaginary point in the future.

And for those of us who are people of faith, we need to keep prayer and silence and compassion and forgiveness at the heart of all of our political wranglings.

I have no idea how we are going to do any of this. But I am certain that if we don't start working together to build a society where contemplation and civility matter more than my side winning at all costs, then the trajectory of the past couple of decades is likely to just keep getting worse.

Even as I am writing these few paragraphs, it has hit me: *I'm not so unique in my fear.*

Sure, maybe most kids have no problem telling grownups what they want to be when they grow up. And most teenagers figure out how to talk to the person they think is irresistibly cute. And most adults learn how to feel the fear and do it anyway, at least in terms of making a living and charting a career.

But it seems that when it comes to how we manage conflict in our lives, whether the big conflicts of politics or the little conflicts of our families, so often the reason why things go awry is because we start making choices out of fear rather than out of trust.

So let me make a deal with you, my dear readers. I want to become a better writer, which includes learning how to write about conflict in a mindful and honest and hopeful way. Your part of the bargain: please join with me in learning how to navigate the conflicts in your life from a place of trust rather than fear.

### Prayer, Generosity, and Trust

One day a few years back, I was reading the writing of Julian of Norwich, the medieval English mystic, and came across this passage in the very first chapter of the book where Julian is describing her sixteen visions or "showings." Here she is commenting on the fourteenth showing, where God teaches her about prayer.

> The fourteenth Revelation is that the Lord God is the ground of our praying. Arising from this, we are shown true prayer and steady trust and God wants us to be generous in both alike. In this way our praying is pleasing to him and in his goodness he fulfills it.[1]

This short little paragraph basically blew my mind.

First, the idea that *trust* is something we can *give*. God asks us to be *generous* in our trust. Likewise with prayer. I understood that generosity is a virtue (even if it were a virtue I mostly lacked). But I always thought of generosity in material ways: being generous with my money or other resources, or maybe my time. It had never occurred to me that refusing to pray basically meant I was being ungenerous in my relationship with God, and, likewise, that refusing to trust God was similarly a withholding of spiritual generosity.

Now, I'm saying these things not to be judgmental toward myself. I know this can sound like I was accusing myself of some moral failing here. But at the moment when I first read these words, they had the opposite effect on me. I didn't feel *judged* for my lack of generosity, but rather I felt *invited* to become a more *trusting* person (something

I have always wanted to be) by learning how to be more *generous* in prayer.

It seemed to me that Julian of Norwich was saying, very simply, something along these lines:

"God is the source of our prayer. When we pray, we're actually giving a gift to God, a gift that comes from God originally—kind of like when a child gives a Christmas present to her parents, even though the parents actually paid for it. Still, the giving is the heart of it. So when we give our prayer generously to God, we become more generous and, therefore, more God-like. Meanwhile, prayer is related to trust. Trust, like prayer, is a gift from God which we are invited to give back to God—generously. The more generous we are, the more that gift becomes *real* in our lives and in our hearts. Therefore prayer and trust are linked: God invites us to be generous in praying to God, which in turn leads to being generous in trusting God. The more prayerful we are, the more trusting we can become. When we pray for God to meet our needs, we can trust that God will do so, for God loves our prayer and responds to us with perfect goodness. Even when we don't get what we think we want, that just means God's wisdom has discerned an even better path for us to follow."

Wow.

I knew I wasn't a very trusting person. I also knew I wasn't a very generous person, and truth be told, not a particularly prayerful person either.

But for the first time, I saw that these three spiritual gifts—all originating in God—are deeply and integrally linked. If I want to be more prayerful, begin by trying to be more generous in my prayer. If I want to be more trusting, begin by praying. And if I want to be more generous, one important first step would be to simply take the risk of trusting.

My amygdala kept trying to find a loophole, a flaw in this plan. But it was elegant in its simplicity, even as it was luminous in its promise. God wants us to be generous, to be trusting, and to be prayerful. And whenever we take a step, *even a baby step*, in the direction of one of these gifts, by grace we simultaneously receive a measure of all three.

Julian of Norwich is by no means the only mystic to have something positive and creative to say about trust. The German Dominican theologian Meister Eckhart once said, "Since no one could ever love God too much, so also no one could ever trust him too much. Nothing that a person can do is so fitting as to have great trust in God. God never ceased to achieve great things through those who ever gained great confidence in him. He has truly shown to all people that this trusting comes from love, for love not only has trust, it also has true knowledge and unshakeable certainty."[2] As Julian linked trust and generosity, so Eckhart links trust and love; furthermore, he offers a delightful promise: that the more we trust God, the more we make ourselves available for God to work miracles through us. That's an exciting thought.

Perhaps an even more useful (at least for me) idea about trust came from the Cistercian abbess Gertrude the Great, "I call it a gift rather than a virtue."[3] In other words, trust is not so much something we have to attain by our own merits, but rather is something we receive from God, by grace.

You want to be more trusting? Ask God for it.

Meanwhile, another Cistercian mystic, Bernard of Clairvaux, said, "We trust the better by seeming not to trust."[4] What on earth could he mean by this? Here's my guess: that trust actually originates in *not trusting*. Think about it. Doctors treat sick people, not well people. You hire a business coach because you want to become more productive at work, not to brag about how productive you already are. In a similar vein, God gives the gift of trust precisely to the people who need it the most, those who have difficulty trusting. It is our lack of trust that makes us available to receive the gift of trust—if only we are willing to open our hearts and say yes to the blessing.

The great Flemish mystic John Ruusbroec wrote, "When a person thus beholds the marvelous richness and sublimity of the divine nature and all the manifold gifts which God offers and gives to his creatures, there grows within him or her an interior sense of wonder at such great and diverse richness and sublimity and at the infinite fidelity which God bears toward his creatures. This gives rise to a special interior joy in the spirit and a sense of great trust in God. This interior joy envelops and penetrates all the powers of the soul and the unity of the spirit."[5]

In other words, the key to receiving the gift of trust from God is the very act of *beholding God*—the practice of contemplation. When we gaze with wordless love into the heart and mind of God, we are making ourselves available for this gift (among others). The "interior sense of wonder" that God bestows upon the person resting in silent love before God is not only a blessing in its own right, but it is also a key to "interior joy"—and the ability to more fully trust in God.

In one of his minor writings, the author of *The Cloud of Unknowing* has this honest comment to make: "As far as you can see, everything has gone—ordinary graces as well as the more special. But you must not be too disturbed, though it seems that you have every reason to be. Rather trust lovingly in our Lord, as much as you can at the time, however feebly; for he is not far off. He will turn his face to you, perhaps very soon, and affect you again with a touch of that same grace more ardently than you ever experienced before."[6]

What an honest statement—acknowledging that sometimes our ability to trust is *feeble*!

I could relate to that. I saw that trusting is almost like working out in a gym. If you're out of practice, you're not going to be able to life much weight—so, start small. Lift what you can, safely, and keep working out; eventually you will gain strength and be able to press more weight. Trust works the same way. At first we are feeble in our trust, but that's better than nothing. And the more we exercise our trust, the more we recognize that God "is not far off" and will turn the divine face to us "soon."

Going back to the earliest Christian centuries, consider these words from the ancient monk John Cassian: "It is borne in upon us that we should pass from fear of punishment to the full freedom of love and to that trust which characterizes the friends and sons of God."[7] Here we see that trust is related not only to generosity, prayer, and love, but also to freedom.

The more we trust, the freer we are.

Lack of trust is actually a form of interior bondage. The key to unlocking those chains is the gift of grace sought through prayer and perseverance.

Finally, let's go back to dear Julian of Norwich, who acknowledged, "often our trust is not complete, for we are not certain that almighty God hears us; . . . often we are as barren and dry after our prayers as we were before. And thus when we feel so, it is our folly which is the cause of our weakness, for I have experienced this in myself. And our Lord brought all this suddenly to my mind, and gave me great strength and vitality to combat this kind of weakness in praying, and said: I am the foundation of your beseeching."[8]

In other words, God encourages us to trust even though we don't know how to trust very well.

Julian doesn't mince words and suggests that our lack of trust is foolishness on our part, but that God offers us strength in response to our weakness. When God says, "I am the foundation of your beseeching," in effect he is saying, "even your *desire* to trust comes from me."

## The Unending Lessons

I've come to see that trust is a lot like love. In fact, I sometimes wonder if trust is simply a different dimension of love. As I write these words, Fran and I have been married twenty-five years, and I feel like I am still learning how to love her. I certainly recognize that, after more than twenty years as Rhiannon's dad, I never came close to learning all the lessons of love that she had to teach me. We never master love, and I suppose even saints have to keep learning how to love as life circumstances change and new challenges (and opportunities) emerge.

Likewise, we never master the art of trusting—of trusting God, of trusting ourselves, of trusting the people in our lives. Sure, some of us are better at trusting than others. But for me at least, making the commitment to live my life oriented toward trust rather than fear has proven to be an ongoing journey. I think this is a lifelong lesson. But God is always at the heart of my schooling in trust, and that, in itself, is a cause for trust.

So what does all this have to do with me learning how to write about conflict?

Don't you see? My resistance to writing about conflict is simply an inner conflict within me.

Likewise, all the current social and political problems that we face as a nation or as a neighborhood, all the challenges that impact our families or our planet require us to become people of deep interior trust in order to respond to the challenges we face. Whether they are big challenges or small. Global, national, or local.

I still don't want to pick sides in my writing, but maybe in the future I'll get a bit bolder talking about an issue, especially when I think there is a particular contemplative way to approach the question. With that approach, I imagine sooner or later I'll get people on all sides of the political spectrum annoyed with me. But if I am writing out of a place of deep trust—and deep love—then hopefully I'll have something to say that can make a difference, at least to some people.

Likewise, if we are distressed by the direction our nation is going, or by the endless litany of character assassinations and mud-slinging in our public conversations, or by the tendency our teenagers have to turn every conversation into an argument, well, perhaps we need to recalibrate how we think about and approach and respond to all of these areas of conflict.

We need to begin with trust. And generosity. And for those of us who believe, with prayer. And most of all, with love.

This is not a panacea, as if we can pray away all our conflicts. One last quotation from Julian of Norwich. In her final mystical vision, Christ tells her, "You shall not be overcome." Julian reflects on what this means: "All this teaching of true comfort applies in general to all my fellow Christians, as is said before, and it is God's will that it is so. And these words, 'You shall not be overcome', were said very distinctly and very powerfully for assurance and comfort against all the tribulations that may come. He did not say, 'You shall not be perturbed, you shall not be troubled, you shall not be distressed', but he said, 'You shall not be overcome.' God wants us to pay attention to these words and always to be trusting strongly and surely in good times and bad; for he loves us and is pleased with us, and so he wishes us to love him, and be pleased with him, and strongly trust in him; and all shall be well."[9]

There it is, my friends. We are not promised a life without conflict. But we are asked to face our inevitable conflicts with trust.

Once I was a frightened little boy who didn't want a dangerous job because I had no idea how to trust God or to trust life or to trust myself. Slowly, over the years, I have little by little learned to trust God and life and myself more and more. This is an unteachable lesson that I am still learning. But every time I remember to choose trust over fear, even the scariest conflicts are transformed into opportunities rather than perils.

There's a Bible verse that proclaims, "Though he slay me, yet will I trust in him" ( Job 13:15 KJV). In other words, "I choose to trust God always and in all circumstances; so that even when life seems to be falling apart, I will continue to trust."

May we all learn this unteachable lesson. Even if it takes us a lifetime—and beyond.

# Epilogue: On Beyond Zebra!

On the day I met Rhiannon, I read her a Dr. Seuss book. I can so vividly remember her smile, the feel of her hand as she tugged on my beard, and the smell of the dinner Fran was preparing as I visited with Rhiannon. But one detail from that auspicious day eludes me. I don't recall which book we read. Sigh. Some secrets memory will not easily yield.

While I don't remember what book I actually read to her, I know what book I would have liked to read to her. That, without a doubt, would be *On Beyond Zebra!*

My reasoning for this is purely selfish: it's my favorite Dr. Seuss book. Okay, *Yertle the Turtle and Other Stories* runs a *very* close second, but *On Beyond Zebra!* remains my favorite—more so than *Green Eggs and Ham* or *Horton Hears a Who* or *The Cat in the Hat* or any other of the wacky doc's best-known books. Admitting that *On Beyond Zebra!* is my favorite Seuss book is rather like admitting that my favorite ice cream flavor is pistachio mint. All the vanilla and chocolate and strawberry lovers look at me like I'm strange. But there's no accounting for taste, and mine has always been a bit offbeat.

*On Beyond Zebra!* features Dr. Seuss's rather bizarro imagining of what the alphabet might look like if it were suddenly supersized, that is to say, if it didn't stop with Z. Envisioning an alphabet with forty-six letters instead of the customary twenty-six, Dr. Seuss invites his readers to imagine new letters with freaky-weird names and sounds, like *Yuzz*, *Glick*, and *Vroo*. As the narrator puts it, "In the places I go there are things that I see that I *never* could spell if I stopped with the Z." And then, "It's high time you were shown that you really *don't* know all there is to be known."

Indeed, by the end of the book, when the reader's mind is sufficiently blown (or perhaps expanded) by all the imaginary letters (and the imaginary creatures whose names are spelled with these letters), Dr. Seuss introduces his readers to a complexly drawn letter that doesn't even have a name. He jokingly says, "What do YOU think we should call this one, anyhow?"

I learned so much from this book. When I was a kid, I couldn't have told you why I loved *On Beyond Zebra!* so much; I couldn't put it into words. (Maybe I didn't have enough words in my vocabulary or letters in my alphabet to explain what was going on within me.) But now I think I can try to express the wonder that I felt as I explored those extra twenty letters in the world of pure make-believe.

*Epilogue: On Beyond Zebra!*

As I went with Dr. Seuss on beyond Z, I learned that language has limits—but those limits do not exhaust all of reality or even all of human knowledge. Even before I could put it into words, I began to sense that knowledge is finite, and beyond the reaches of verbal, logical knowledge we find, well, we find mystery, mystery luminous with wonder, mystery that only silence can fully contain or fully reveal. And I learned that it seems to be something of the human condition to push against the boundaries of knowledge and the limits of language because we want to explore whatever it is that is out there, out there in the mystery, or perhaps I should say *in there,* in the mystery deep within.

You see, *On Beyond Zebra!* takes us not into the far reaches of outer space or the hidden jungles of some exotic faraway land, but rather to what might well be the most amazing and unexplored frontier of all—the wilderness deep within, far below and beyond and above the most extreme reaches of abstract thought and symbolic or conceptual language. The only way to access this frontier is through silence. Monks and mystics have been exploring it for millennia now, but it doesn't just belong to Zen masters or advanced contemplatives. That place beyond the last letter is hidden within each of us, and no one can show it to you. You have to find it for yourself. What makes a Tibetan lama or Christian saint or Sufi master or (for that matter) Dr. Seuss so indispensable is that they give us clues about where to look. But still, the treasure hunt is all our own. No one can do it for us.

I've joked with people when they've asked me about the book I'm writing these days. I say, "It's a book about how you can't learn everything from a book." But even just saying that is something of a paradox. It's like the statement "This is a lie." If that statement is true, then it is false; but if it is false, then it is true.

What does it mean to write a book about the fact that spirituality can't (ultimately) be learned from a book? If I'm really suggesting that books aren't necessary, then I'm out of a job. But the analogy goes like this: the map is not the territory, but we still need maps if for no other reason than to guide us to the territory we ultimately must explore for ourselves. Likewise, spiritual books (and spiritual teachers) can never replace the importance of simply living into the lessons that life alone can give us: lessons about grief and silence and embodiment and love and trust—you know, the stuff we've been looking at together over the course of this book. But hopefully good books and teachers still have a function in our lives akin to the place that maps have in the backpacks of explorers. Our guides and teachers and sacred texts help to orient us, to point us in the directions we would like to go.

We still need to go—to do the work of living, of praying, of loving, of trusting, of listening to the silence—for ourselves.

There are two dangers we must take care to avoid. The first danger is to simply refuse to do our own work and just live vicariously through the wisdom and experience of others. But the second danger is to discard or reject the wisdom of those who have gone before us and insist that doing our own work is all that matters.

Spiritually speaking, when we make the first mistake, we settle for a religion of dogma and ritual but no living spiritual heart. But when we make the second mistake, we become spiritual narcissists, refusing to integrate our own spiritual life with the shared wisdom and experience of all who have gone before us.

This, my friends, is the end of the map. I've said pretty much all that I think I can say, at least for now. Writing is something of an addiction, so I'm sure I'll be back for more—if not another book, then at least more posts to my blog. I hope I'll see you around.

Read good books—but then put them down. One of my first prayer teachers used to say, "Reading about prayer is one of the sneakiest ways we have of actually avoiding prayer." Please keep that in mind. So do your homework: get to know the mystics and contemplatives of Christianity and of the world, and get to know what the explorers ahead of you have to say about their journey. But then the time will come when you need to close the book and go on beyond zebra with only your heart as your guide.

I wish you much joy and many adventures in your search.

## ACKNOWLEDGMENTS

The idea for this book was born out of two conversations that occurred decades apart.

When I was a senior in high school, someone I knew from church, Steve Ikenberry, noticed that I was a bookworm. One time we were chatting about spiritual matters, and he made a pointed remark: "You know, the answers you are seeking you won't find in a book." That was my first on-beyond-zebra moment of realizing that some of life's most important lessons cannot be taught, at least not by ordinary teachers or the written word.

Years later, I was chatting with Lil Copan, the editor who worked with me on *Befriending Silence*. We were talking about ideas for my next book, and when I mentioned to her this notion "that the most important spiritual lessons can't be learned from a book," she responded with enthusiasm. *Unteachable Lessons* is the result.

My gratitude goes to Steve and Lil, along with Linda Roghaar, James D. Ernest, and everyone at William B.

Eerdmans for their contribution to making this book a reality.

Portions of the book originally appeared on my blog, which can be found at www.patheos.com/blogs/carlmccolman.

I am richly blessed to be able to devote much of my time to research and writing, thanks in part to the generous support I receive from benefactors through Patreon, a crowdfunding platform for creative professionals.

As always, words cannot express my gratitude for Fran McColman, my wife, my best friend, and my most dedicated unteaching teacher, who daily invites me to live from the heart rather than the head. As for Rhiannon, who lives not only in heaven but also in my heart, all I can say is *Gonzo loves you!*

CARL MCCOLMAN
*Feast of the Epiphany 2019*

# NOTES

## Prologue: A Cat by the Tail

1. Benedict of Nursia, *The Rule of St. Benedict in English* 6.2, ed. Timothy Fry et al. (Collegeville, MN: Liturgical Press, 1982).

2. I'll have more to say on the silence of God later in this book; for now I just want to point out that many Christians seem to prefer a God who speaks to them.

3. This basic idea is found in Mark Twain, *Tom Sawyer Abroad* (Salt Lake City: Project Gutenberg, 2018).

4. N. T. Wright, *The Challenge of Jesus* (Downers Grove, IL: InterVarsity Press, 2015), loc. 2504-6, Kindle.

## The Unteachable Lessons

1. Throughout Rhiannon's life, she would link us to favorite characters from movies or TV shows she loved. After the first *Shrek* movie came out, she decided she was the Donkey and I was Shrek (and Fran, Princess Fiona). Even well into her twenties, we were still playing roles: she was Kermit the Frog, I was Gonzo the Great (and poor Fran, stuck with being Gonzo's sweetheart, was Camilla the Chicken).

2. I was writing *Befriending Silence* (Notre Dame, IN: Ave Maria Press, 2015) when Rhiannon was in hospice, and doing the research for *Christian Mystics* (Charlottesville, VA: Hampton Roads, 2016).

## Feeling It in the Bones (or Not)

1. I first wrote about this in my book *The Aspiring Mystic: Practical Steps for Spiritual Seekers* (Avon, MA: Adams Media, 2000).

2. Thomas Merton once wrote, after his own moment of epiphany, "There is no way of telling people that they are all walking around shining like the sun." I think I might know what he was talking about. (See Merton's *Conjectures of a Guilty Bystander*, Kindle edition [New York: Random House, 2009], 153–56.)

3. Dennis Bennett and Rita Bennett, *The Holy Spirit and You* (Alachua, FL: Bridge Logos, 1989), 69–70.

4. Julian of Norwich, *Revelations of Divine Love*, Oxford World's Classics (Oxford: Oxford University Press, 2015), 51–52, Kindle.

## The Page on Which the Words Are Written

1. The manuscripts of Julian's writings show her visions as occurring either on May "VIII" or May "XIII" in the year 1373. We're not sure which is correct and which is a scribe's error. So her visions happened on either the eighth or the thirteenth. As a confirmed Julian nerd, I just celebrate both days.

2. I'm not exactly sure why I want to personify silence as feminine, but I think it might have to do with the fact that in Aramaic (the language Jesus spoke), the Spirit is feminine.

3. Ken Wilber, *A Brief History of Everything* (Boston: Shambhala, 2000), 211, Kindle.

4. Thomas Keating, *Invitation to Love*, 20th anniv. ed. (New York: Bloomsbury Continuum, 2012), 105.

5. Rabbi Rami, quoted on the home page of rabbirami.com, accessed July 17, 2018.

6. *Lectio divina* is an ancient monastic practice of reading Scripture in a slow, meditative way, leading to prayer and ultimately to contemplation.

### That Word, "I Do Not Think It Means
### What You Think It Means"

1. The person who commented on my blog was probably inspired by an atheist named Marshall Fields, whose website www .whywontgodhealamputees.com apparently has become popular among some nonbelievers because of its clever mix of logic, sarcasm, and aggression.

### Pagans and Druids and Buddhists—Oh My!

1. Kenneth Leech, *Soul Friend*, rev. ed. (Harrisburg, PA: Morehouse, 2001). Nowadays, books like *Soul Friend* seem almost obsolete because the language is very stiff, academic, and gender-exclusive (when Ken wrote the book in the 1970s, he thought only priests would read it, and at that time only men could be Anglican priests). I think this just shows how far the literature of contemporary spirituality has come in the last fifty years. Although I did not know Ken intimately, I certainly can attest that his use of gendered language was just a product of when he was writing; he himself was very affirming of women in ministry, priestly or otherwise.

2. P. E. I. Bonewits, *Real Magic* (Newburyport, MA: Weiser, 1989), vii.

3. Witchcraft is like meditation: a practitioner need not have any formal religious affiliation. But both witchcraft and meditation are associated with religious cultures that are based upon them: so you could say a Buddhist is someone who practices meditation in

a religious context; likewise a Wiccan is someone who practices witchcraft in a religious context.

4. At this point I suppose I should acknowledge that there are some Christians, typically of a conservative evangelical mind, who think being a pagan and being a Catholic are both equally bad. Chances are, however, that such people are not very likely to read my books or attend one of my talks, so my dealing with such persons is, thank heaven, limited.

5. Catholic Church, *Catechism of the Catholic Church*, 2nd ed. (Vatican: Libreria Editrice Vaticana, 2000), paragraph 856, page 2227.

6. "Dialogue and Proclamation," *The Vatican*, accessed November 26, 2018, http://www.vatican.va/roman_curia/pontifical_councils /interelg/documents/rc_pc_interelg_doc_19051991_dialogue -and-proclamatio_en.html.

## Let Him Kiss Me with the Kisses of His Mouth

1. I double checked just to see if someone had written a book with a title like that. At least as of early 2019, no one had—although there are a few websites with that title. Just goes to show you can find anything online.

## It's the End of the World as We Know It (and I Feel Fine)

1. Julian of Norwich, *Revelations of Divine Love*, ed. Halcyon Backhouse and Rhona Pipe (London: Hodder & Stoughton, 1987), 4.

2. Meister Eckhart, *Meister Eckhart: The Essential Sermons, Commentaries, Treatises, and Defense,* ed. Richard J. Payne, trans. Edmund Colledge and Bernard McGinn (Mahwah, NJ: Paulist Press, 1981), 263. I've edited this passage slightly to make the language more inclusive.

3. Gertrude of Helfta, *The Herald of Divine Love*, ed. Margaret

Winkworth and Bernard McGinn, trans. Margaret Winkworth (Mahwah, NJ: Paulist Press, 1993), 68.

4. Bernard of Clairvaux, *Bernard of Clairvaux: Selected Works*, ed. John Farina, trans. G. R. Evans (Mahwah, NJ: Paulist Press, 1987), 140.

5. John Ruusbroec, *John Ruusbroec: The Spiritual Espousals and Other Works*, ed. John Farina, trans. J. A. Wiseman (Mahwah, NJ: Paulist Press 1985), 102. I've edited this passage slightly to make the language more inclusive.

6. James A. Walsh, ed., *The Pursuit of Wisdom and Other Works by the Author of the Cloud of Unknowing*, trans. James A. Walsh (New York: Paulist Press, 1988), 244.

7. John Cassian, *John Cassian: Conferences*, ed. John Farina, trans. Colm Luibheid (Mahwah, NJ: Paulist Press, 1985), 152–53.

8. Julian of Norwich, *Julian of Norwich: Showings*, ed. Richard J. Payne, trans. Edmund Colledge and James Walsh (Mahwah, NJ: Paulist Press, 1978), 157.

9. Julian of Norwich, *Revelations of Divine Love*, Oxford World's Classics (Oxford: Oxford University Press, 2015), 143, Kindle.